ADVANCE PRAISE FOR
SPARK BRILLIANCE

"Insightful and practical! Jackie has perfectly illustrated how you can be using Positive Psychology in leadership to inspire, engage, and transform your team and work culture. Read this book, take its advice, and redefine the way you lead!"

—Marshall Goldsmith, Thinkers 50 #1 Executive Coach and
New York Times #1 bestselling author of
Triggers, Mojo, and *What Got You Here Won't Get You There*

"Insightful, compassionate, and timely...Jackie does what brilliant teachers do best: she starts with a deep well of understanding and empathy to then guide the reader through her knowledge of Positive Psychology to culminate in practical ways to spark lasting positive change at work and at home. Spark Brilliance *is not just about seeking positive change in your life, but catalyzing change in your entire ecosystem."*

—Shawn Achor, *New York Times* bestselling author of
The Happiness Advantage and Big Potential

"Spark Brilliance *is an inspiring read for how we can be accountable leaders through the use of Positive Psychology. Jackie Insinger's approach is transformative and practical. Prepare to take notes!"*

—Hannah Gordon, Chief Administrative Officer and General Counsel, San Francisco 49ers

"In working with Jackie professionally and personally for nearly five years, I have gained countless sparks of brilliance on how to show up as a better leader and human. This book uses research and real-life wisdom to outline for leaders a winning formula for inspiring their teams and driving higher performance. Platinum Leadership has allowed me to engage with my team with the utmost connection, creativity, and joy. This practical playbook for leaders is brilliantly simple and simply brilliant."

—Eileen Moore Johnson, CHRO of Scientific Games, former Regional President of Caesars Entertainment

"Leaders often position themselves to have all the answers—but the best leaders continually search for greater learning and potential. Jackie has always been a thought leader, and with Spark Brilliance, *she gives you a guide to learn more, lead better, and shine brighter."*

—Dolvett Quince, *New York Times* bestselling author, self-development coach, and TV personality

"The first line of this book is, 'It begins with you'—and that couldn't be more true. Jackie Insinger's positive and actionable concepts have been game-changing for our leaders and organization. Spark Brilliance *is different from every other leadership book you've read. It's smart. It's relatable. It's strategic. And it works."*

—Sara Gelenberg-Field, former Vice President and Head of Marketing at Nestlé Coffee Partners

"*Jackie has managed to codify the complex world of leadership and human nature into a practical approach to creating high performance. As we design the future of work and deal with the challenges of a hybrid world, this book is as valuable to the CEO as it is to the frontline manager.*"

−Peter Sheahan, bestselling author, thought leader, CEO, and C-suite advisor

"*Jackie's Brilliance should be read by everyone in a leadership role. She masterfully illustrates how great leaders create authentic connections to foster trust, safety, and results. By investing in those foundational relationships, individuals will find their own brilliance and bring it out in others. I have adapted my own leadership style after reading* Spark Brilliance *and am already seeing more engaged and fulfilled colleagues.*"

−Jason Trevisan, CEO, CarGurus

"*Jackie's perspective is simultaneously simple and revelatory. This is a treasure chest of practical wisdom that will accelerate your journey to becoming an inspiring and confident leader.*"

−Joe Mechlinski, *New York Times* Bestselling Author and CEO of SHIFT

"*Sharp, practical, and extremely useful. Imagine building a team where employees wake up inspired to work together, feel safe when they are there, and feel fulfilled by the work they do.* Spark Brilliance *provides valuable foundational principles to building such a team, and is filled with illustrative examples and concrete steps to elevate your leadership journey. Jackie has taken her years of experience working with clients and teams to put together a roadmap for those in a leadership position.*"

−Tracy Tobin, Chief People Officer, Adswerve

"The skills I've learned from Jackie have transformed my professional (and personal) trajectory. Using the tools in Spark Brilliance, *I've been able to embrace my best and authentic self as a leader, tailoring my style to support individual team members. I've learned how to ask the right questions, understand what makes employees feel happy, motivated and valued, and listen to what is being said—and not said—to create a trusting, fun, and high-performing environment. I'm better able to create extraordinary teams by using the incredibly practical and immediately actionable strategies in* Spark Brilliance.*"*

–Tisha Pedrazzini, President and Executive Principal Officer, SLG-Inc., and former President, The Integer Group

"Jackie is the only business coach I've worked with who concentrates in the field of Positive Psychology, the place where we become our best selves and inspire those around us. The natural high that comes from operating above our baseline is a feeling like no other. This book sparks that journey for leaders, opening doors to endless potential."

–Reinier Santana, President, Ovation

"Anyone who strives to be the best version of themselves will love this book. The insights in Spark Brilliance *are universal, and that's what makes them so powerful. Jackie will inspire you and give you the tools to achieve greatness in yourself, in others, and most importantly, on the team you serve or lead."*

–Helen Drexler, CEO, Ensemble Innovation Ventures and President, Delta Dental of Colorado

"Jackie has been sparking brilliance within our team for years. Spark Brilliance *provides practical tips you and your team can use every day to foster better communication and a more positive culture where people feel heard and valued for their unique contributions. Jackie has been integral to our evolution, and I credit her for our sanity and our success!"*

—Gem Swartz, CEO, Catalyst Marketing Agency

"Spark Brilliance *is a must-read. After engaging Jackie as my Executive Coach and employing the strategies she shares in this book, my team watched a spark ignite a flame that has built into a blaze of valuable returns, momentum, and company enthusiasm. Can Jackie's positive and actionable strategies yield great results? We're living proof that they can: our company has grown 81 percent since we started working with her. Jackie is a veritable Swiss army knife of practices and solutions for creating high-performance teams and leaders."*

—Joel Grabois, CEO, Blue Onion Media

"Jackie's Brilliance *breaks through the mystery on how to be an effective leader with a step-by-step playbook that helps you identify and ignite the spark that lives in each individual on your team.* Spark Brilliance *breaks down the often overwhelming messiness of leadership into digestible, easy-to-understand practices you can apply immediately. What seems difficult and complex, Jackie makes incredibly manageable and exciting—for both leaders and teams."*

—Dana Benfeld, CMO Wellness Division, WellBiz Brands

"Spark Brilliance *is the roadmap to becoming a more emotionally intelligent and empathetic leader. Through relatable, well-researched, and actionable insights, Jackie clearly illustrates how to create a culture full of empowered, passionate, and highly fulfilled employees to take your organization to the next level. This is a required read for the modern-day CEO.*"

—Ben Kaplan, CEO and Dreamer, Collective Goods, Books Are Fun, and Power of Purpose ("PoP!")

"The strength of Jackie's work with team dynamics and leaders is that her methods consistently move from insights to real-world advice. She's captured both in Spark Brilliance*: new ways to see yourself and your teammates, and a practical playbook to unlock the hidden power of your organization."*

—Matt Holford, Senior Director of Engineering, Etsy

"Spark Brilliance *offers a truly fresh approach to what it means to find and be your personal best. Jackie's methodology reminds me to do better for myself and others, every day, using my own spark."*

—Angie Tebbe, CEO, Rae Wellness

SPARK
BRILLIANCE

A LEADER'S PLAYBOOK

SPARK
BRILLIANCE

HOW THE SCIENCE OF POSITIVE
PSYCHOLOGY WILL IGNITE, ENGAGE,
AND TRANSFORM YOUR TEAM

JACKIE INSINGER

LIONCREST
PUBLISHING

SPARK BRILLIANCE

How the Science of Positive Psychology Will Ignite, Engage, and Transform Your Team

ISBN   978-1-5445-2709-3   *Hardcover*

        978-1-5445-2710-9   *Paperback*

        978-1-5445-2711-6   *Ebook*

For Kelley, our fierce and fabulous party angel
and the most brilliant light I have ever known.

One of the greatest gifts I have ever received was my promise to you.

Thank you for showing me just how much my voice really matters.
I am eternally grateful for you and I miss you every single day.

CONTENTS

INTRODUCTION

"It begins with you."

This might not be *exactly* what you want to hear when you're having an emotional breakdown in a coaching session, but that day, it was the beginning of a seismic shift for the person who was hearing it.

I'd been working one-on-one with Lauren for several months. Like so many leaders I count as clients and friends, Lauren was whip-smart, snappy, ambitious, the kind of person who'd always raised her hand first and run headlong into the fray in life. A forty-two-year-old single mom and Ivy League grad, she was funny and wise, charismatic and competent. Her career as a top executive at a Fortune 500 software company had been set on a steep upward trajectory; in the span of five years, she'd gone from mid-level employee to the leadership team. She'd risen to the challenge of each new level she unlocked with passion and determination. She wanted to be the best strategist, the most productive collaborator, the most effective leader. And for a while, she was.

Then, somewhere along the way, something shifted. She didn't notice it until her once-steady footing suddenly began to feel shaky.

One day, there was an oddly biting comment from a coworker, the next day a whisper behind her back from another. A direct report quit, citing a lack of fulfillment.

The wind was changing, so subtly at first that it had taken her by surprise.

"I used to love all my coworkers, my peers. It used to feel totally different. I don't know what changed."

Lauren had sought out my coaching to help with what she perceived as an altered reality, a workplace where the people who had once been open, eager creative partners had become competitors. With each new promotion she'd achieved, the distance between people she'd once felt so connected to felt like it had widened more and more. Her former peers had become territorial and distrusting, guarding their information where they'd once shared, withholding cooperation where they'd once opened their arms to her.

She knew that this was partly the normal course of rising in the corporate ranks. The higher she climbed the pyramid, the fewer roles there were at each level, creating competition for those higher-level roles where once it had seemed like there was room for everyone.

Even though she recognized this scarcity effect, the feeling of being seen as an outright threat was new to her. And it was stressing her out.

Worse, it was stressing her *team* out. Everyone felt the discord, the bad vibes. With the leadership team of the organization stuck in a downward spiral of competitiveness and mistrust, many of the employees were beginning to mirror its effects in their work and interactions. Productivity dipped; engagement was evaporating. The energy of the workplace had taken a sharp dive, like bubbles dissipating from a can of soda left to go flat.

It's not fun anymore, Lauren kept hearing, both in formal check-ins and overheard lunch conversations.

She felt a panicked sense that she was failing her own team, the people she led and cared so much about. She went into detective mode, determined to find the problem and fix what was wrong. *I can't do anything about the leadership culture, but at least I can lead my own people.* The more she tried to find the reason things felt like they were falling apart, the more desperate she became.

"Why can't I see what's wrong? What am I supposed to do?" These were the questions I heard from her over the months we worked together. Before my eyes, she seemed to fade more and more into herself with each session we had; the once vibrant, energetic brunette lost her glow. Her stress and unhappiness were like a cloud around her that got darker as the weeks went on.

Until that day, when the cloudburst I'd been anticipating finally happened.

Lauren had signed on for our video session, looked straight into the webcam, and announced stoically, "I think I've decided to quit." Then she immediately burst into tears.

It wasn't the first time or even the hundredth time I've held space for a client while they spent several minutes sobbing out the worry, the fear, the stress and disappointment of it all. Being a leader, after all, often feels isolating. It can feel like there's no one else with the same pressures, burdens, and responsibilities.

I let Lauren take the time she needed to feel the feelings. I've learned over many years of coaching clients that it's crucial to be quiet and listen fully while they pour it all out.

"I hate how I'm feeling," she said brokenly. "I've worked so hard to get here, and I don't want to give up, but I hate how I feel. I'm so unfulfilled. I hate how I'm showing up. This is not how I work. *This is not who I am.*"

When the clouds began to lift, she looked at me, wiping away the last of the rapidly drying tears, and asked the crucial question.

"What do I do?"

And I replied, "Think positive!"

No, I didn't. But that's where a lot of people's minds go when they hear the term *Positive Psychology*, so I thought I'd get it out of the way right off the bat: this isn't a book about positive thinking. Lauren wasn't going to be helped by trite encouragement to look for the silver lining, see the sunny side, and so on.

This is a book about brilliance.

Brilliance in all aspects of our experience as leaders: our relationships, our talent, our performance, our outlook.

Brilliance in our work, that is amplified when we come together as a team.

Brilliance that begins with one spark.

What Lauren wasn't seeing, what was so obscured by the unhappiness, stress, and fear, was the enormous opportunity and potential of her situation. Her team was falling apart, and it was because they were following her lead. Her perspective, that something was *wrong* with the workplace, that friends had become adversaries, that trust was in short supply and collaboration was a distant dream, was what her team was mirroring.

I broke the hard truth to her.

"It begins with you."

But that hard truth was also her greatest opportunity.

Her team was following her lead. It was in a direction she didn't like, yes, but the important part was that they *had* followed her there, and they would follow her in a new direction.

If she could change her perspective, she could lead them back to brilliance.

WHERE IT BEGINS

Positive Psychology is the scientific study of what makes life most worth living.

This is a short definition of a field that is more defined by its broadness and potential than by any attempt to contain it within a few succinct words.

What I love about this definition is that it is itself open and far-reaching, making space for a multitude of interpretations, endless avenues of impact.

However, my own work in motivation, communication, executive coaching, and team dynamics over the past two decades has shown me that pinning down a singular definition of Positive Psychology is a bit of a losing game. It's also not the point; Positive Psychology is premised upon expansion, not reduction.

So, how do I define Positive Psychology when asked by friends, colleagues, and clients? The simple answer is that I don't. I prefer to describe it.

Picture a line of numbers with zero in the middle, negative numbers to the left, and positive numbers to the right. When we typically think of our "baseline" as individuals—our sea level of happiness, performance, engagement, and perspective—we place it at zero on the line. When we're feeling low in these areas, we dip below the baseline into the negative numbers.

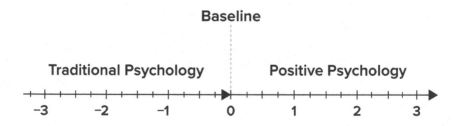

Traditional psychology is the study of those dips, and the practice of healing by bringing people out of the negative numbers back up to their baseline. That's the goal: equilibrium, sea level.

But there's an infinite stretch of positive numbers extending past baseline. How does one keep moving forward?

Positive Psychology is the study and practice of the positive numbers. To me, it's not an *alternative* or *contrast* to traditional psychology; rather, it's a continuation of its impact, the "what's next" sought by a person who has achieved equilibrium. The absence of negative doesn't equal positive; the absence of sickness doesn't equal health. When it comes to your mindset, the absence of sadness doesn't equal happiness. When it comes to your team, the absence of poor performance doesn't equal great performance. Neutral is merely the starting point where great things become possible—not the final destination.

And yet so often, we're stuck in neutral. I see this day after day, not only in my work but with people in my life as well—everyone from friends to family to strangers in the grocery store. I see behaviors and attitudes that suggest a belief that neutral is all we can hope for. Surviving, not thriving. *Happy* is quite a reach; let's just get to *not sad* and call it good, okay?

The father of Positive Psychology, Martin Seligman, carved out the field in the late 1990s as a rebuttal to that idea. President of the American Psychological Association at the time, Seligman introduced a focus on "building what's strong," not just "fixing what's wrong." After coauthoring with Mihaly Csikszentmihalyi the foundational paper on this idea, "Positive Psychology," in 2000,[1] Seligman set out to create what he described as the "positive counterpart" to the *Diagnostic and Statistical Manual of Mental Disorders* (you probably know it as the DSM).

---

1   Martin E. P. Seligman and Mihaly Csikszentmihalyi, "Positive Psychology: An Introduction," *American Psychologist* 55 no. 1 (2000): 5–14,0p https://psycnet.apa.org/doiLanding?-doi=10.1037%2F0003-066X.55.1.5.

The result, Seligman and psychologist Christopher Peterson's *Character Strengths and Virtues: A Handbook and Classification*,[2] became the seminal text in a new field of scientific inquiry: what goes *right*, rather than *wrong*, with people's psychology. What uplifts, inspires, ignites. The study of flourishing, rather than suffering.

Looking back from the lofty perch of my 2022-era thinking, it strikes me as amazing that we went so long as curious beings focused on studying the negative in the field of psychology, rather than the positive. But then, as humans, we're hardwired to focus on survival, which involves doggedly seeking out the *bad* in order to fix or avoid it. Biologically, our cognitive bias is to see the negative—because, sure, that shadow over in the corner of our cave *might* be nothing, but it also might be a bear. We wouldn't have survived as a species if we *didn't* treat every shadow like a bear.

But in our modern world, seeing the bear in every shadow actually holds us back. We now have the privilege and the opportunity to choose *not* to see the bear.

Having studied, worked, and coached in this field for over twenty years, I'm the beneficiary of thousands of scientific studies and publications in the field of Positive Psychology. I studied traditional psychology in both my undergraduate and graduate programs, and I knew I wanted to bring it into my work. My natural state of being, however, has always been optimistic and opportunity-focused, and the study of traditional psychology had me sitting in the negative numbers much of the time. It was fascinating from a scientific perspective—but it didn't align with my passion or mindset.

---

2   Christopher Peterson and Martin E. P. Seligman, *Character Strengths and Virtues: A Handbook and Classification* (New York: American Psychological Association/Oxford University Press, 2004).

I see the stretch of numbers to the right of zero as a road of endless potential. In those positive numbers is joy; creativity; fulfillment; excitement. It's where we experience the deepest connections with each other and where we show up best for everyone in our lives. It's where our performance multiplies and shines outward, not just as individuals, but as teams.

That's where I chose to ground my own practice: helping leaders and professional teams expand their performance by focusing in on their motivation, outlook, and interpersonal connection.

When I'm working with a client and I see the *click* moment, the moment when they shift from neutral into positive, it's the most rewarding feeling in the world. In that moment, their eyes open to the full extent of that infinite line of positive numbers. Their potential unfolds before them, bright and brilliant.

THE PLATINUM RULE

Above all, Positive Psychology is about perspective.

Its greatest benefit, and its greatest potential, lie in its foundational premise that we have power over our perspective, that it's something we can observe, consider, and change. We can choose how we see and experience the world. We can choose how we show up in each moment.

This is incredibly important for how we show up in our interactions with other people. If each of us has a perspective that is fluid rather than fixed, this means there is no one "right" perspective. Each person's perspective is unique and equally valid.

You're probably thinking: *this isn't news.*

And you're right. It's one of those things we hear constantly—*everyone has their own perspective.* Sure. That's a given.

Then why don't we live that way?

So much of our behavior and interactions as a society speak to the opposite belief, that perception is fixed, and that reality *is* our perception. We perceive something, and *that's how it happened.* We focus inward on our personal experience of each moment and guard our perspective like it's the key piece of evidence in the trial of the century.

This self-focus imbues not only our actions but also our guidelines for interaction. For example, take one of the most well-known "rules" for how to interact with other people: the Golden Rule.

Treat others the way you want to be treated.

Key word: *you.* The way *you* want to be treated.

Who says the way you want to be treated is the way everyone else wants to be treated?

You know that one well-meaning family member who's just a little out of touch, and when the holidays roll around, they hand out gifts that are what they themselves would *love* to receive, but that leave the recipients befuddled? A ten-year-old unwrapping a coffee table book on Venetian architecture—that's what comes to mind when I think of the Golden Rule.

The Golden Rule is premised on the assumption that your personal perspective is the same as everyone else's. That your deepest wants and needs are exactly the same as the deepest wants and needs of everyone you interact with.

Putting it that way, it's obvious why it doesn't work very well, isn't it?

I once worked with a client, James, who struggled with connecting with one team member in particular. "No matter how much I show her I appreciate her, she never seems to internalize it," he told me.

I asked him to elaborate on what showing her appreciation looked like. "I give her tons of responsibility and ownership, and I point her out to others as the go-to person for questions and expertise. I often refer to her in front of the whole company as not just my right hand, but my right hand, left hand, and both legs."

Interesting—it sounded to me a lot like what James had always said made *him* feel valued. "How often do you simply tell her she's doing a great job, and that you appreciate her?" I asked.

James looked confused. "I do. I told you—I always talk to people about how much I rely on her."

I shook my head. "That's not the same thing. When's the last time you told *her,* instead of everyone else but her?"

"Isn't that a little condescending? I mean, she's not a child—she's a professional. She doesn't want a gold star or a pat on the back."

Working with James more, I got him to see that maybe *he* saw direct verbal affirmations as unnecessary, but it might be exactly how someone else wanted to be recognized. And, lo and behold, the first time he tried simply telling his team member in words that he appreciated her: "She got the biggest smile on her face. I don't think I've ever seen her so happy!"

The Golden Rule keeps us focused on our own wants and needs, when as leaders, our success lies in the wants and needs of the people we serve. Yet the Golden Rule is still at the top of the list when we talk about best practices in relationships. We *know* our own perspective isn't the same as everyone else's, but we follow a practice that keeps us focused on ourselves, rather than the people we're trying to connect with.

Early on in grad school, before I would start to develop the model I would later introduce to thousands of people, I came across a different rule: the Platinum Rule.

It was so simple, and at the same time, it blew my mind.

Treat other people the way they want to be treated.

I thought, *Oh wow, that's genius!*

Then in the next split second, I thought: *Well, duh. Of course.*

It was a strange, dissonant moment. My brain seemed to be having a breakthrough on a new concept, and yet when I really thought about it, it was so obvious that I assumed I must already know it.

That odd feeling of an idea being simultaneously so fresh and yet so familiar is something you'll encounter frequently as you make your way through this book. You'll feel like you've seen some of these concepts before. But through the framework of leadership mindsets and actions

I'm going to present to you, it will also feel revolutionary. Most importantly, it will feel *achievable*. You can definitely do this.

This book is biased toward action. My goal is for you to have a clear series of steps to take after each chapter to immediately spark brilliance in your team.

When sitting down to write this book, I decided *not* to belabor the science behind these concepts. I've done that work for you—this book is where you reap the benefits of my research and study.

You're going to learn the key takeaways from Positive Psychology and how they can most benefit your interactions, not only as a leader, but as a human. Step by step, you'll learn a framework of actions that you can put into practice *right now* with your team. You'll read real-life stories of how the clients I've worked with have moved themselves and their teams into the stretch of numbers to the right of zero, and continue to joyfully expand into their full potential.

The Platinum Rule is where you'll begin, and it's the common thread that weaves through the entire practice you're about to learn.

Your job as a leader is to seek to understand each individual you serve, to authentically connect with them, and to discover *their* perspective. With this discovery, you can treat them how *they* want to be treated—and watch them flourish in response. This is what I call Platinum Leadership.

The Platinum Rule works because it reaches in and grabs hold of one of our deepest desires as humans:

We want to be *known*.

ONE SPARK

When I helped Lauren see the opportunity in what she was experiencing, it was the turning point not only for herself as an individual, but also for her team.

Together, we focused first on her own brilliance. Lauren's leadership style was highly personal, relational, collaborative. She felt most in flow while connecting one-on-one with her team members. She thrived as a mentor and coach. She'd been pulled away from this style of leadership in recent months as she fought battles on two fronts—worrying about the disintegrating culture of the leadership team she was a part of, while scrambling to figure out why her team was losing its cohesion, and how to fix it. She was wholly focused on what was "wrong," what was "missing."

So, we started by bringing it back to her brilliance, her personal spark. Instead of seeing her team as one homogenous group to be fixed, we focused on each individual, and set forth a series of practical steps she could take with each person to grow her connection with them, figure out their spark, and discover their unique needs.

Lauren was on board, but that didn't mean she didn't have her doubts.

"How can I have enough time—let alone enough attention—for each individual on such a close, consistent basis?"

I encouraged her to just try. "What you've been doing isn't working, right? These strategies aren't super time consuming; you can accomplish all these steps in the time you're already spending with your team members. Let's just give it three months and see what you can do with your people."

Nobody reaches Lauren's level of career success by doing things halfway, so I wasn't surprised when, in our next session just one month later, she reported back the extent to which she had attacked her new practice with determination and passion.

The results were obvious, even in just thirty days: her team had started showing noticeable improvements in engagement, collaboration, and happiness. They seemed fueled by a new drive. Their outlook started shifting from pessimistic to optimistic. Three months later, they were outperforming other teams in the organization, and the leadership team was taking notice.

What's going on over there? Lauren had begun to hear from other leaders, the same peers with whom she'd been so stuck in a pattern of dysfunction.

Most of all, her own perspective had begun its seismic shift, and her team was following her in her new direction. She was choosing, moment by moment, not to see the bear. She was choosing to see opportunity and potential. She was sparking in her team the very thing she'd felt was "missing"—her brilliance was their brilliance.

What Lauren was able to achieve is what I've seen countless clients achieve. With this book, you can achieve it too.

And in doing so, you'll not only transform your own leadership and the performance of your team; you'll also skyrocket results for your entire organization. You'll see higher performance in innovation, collaboration, employee engagement, and ultimately, revenue and profit.

The method you're going to learn is simple, and it works.

That said, it's not easy. It takes time. It takes commitment. And then it becomes a mindset shift.

The perspective you choose creates emotional contagion. It ripples through your team, person to person. As the leader, you set the culture with your perspective; you can choose a mindset and outlook that travels like a spark, leaving brilliance in its wake.

You can spark connection, creativity, and joy in your team. You can choose your perspective moment by moment, and it will become second nature.

It's going to require extra effort of you now, but that extra effort will pay massive dividends in the future.

It begins with you.

Great leaders develop strengths.
Exceptional leaders develop sparks.

1

DISCOVER

According to a Salesforce Research survey of 1,500 employees, people who feel seen and heard by their leaders are over four times more motivated to do their best work and perform to the best of their abilities.[3]

"Am I going to get fired?"

Despite her best effort to contain it, Emily's jaw dropped.

This was the absolute *last* thing she would have expected to hear from one of her top project managers, a fiercely organized and outgoing five-year employee named Keisha. In fact, in her coaching sessions with me, Emily often mentioned Keisha as one of the best performers on her team.

Keisha had asked for time on Emily's calendar a week before. Leading up to the one-on-one, Emily had been able to tell Keisha was nervous. Her normally sunny friendliness seemed to be in the shade; she avoided

---

3   Naz Beheshti, "10 Timely Statistics about the Connection between Employee Engagement and Wellness," *Forbes*, January 16, 2019, https://www.forbes.com/sites/nazbeheshti/2019/01/16/10-timely-statistics-about-the-connection-between-employee- engagement-and-well-ness/?sh=2a5f332f22a0.

Emily's eyes when they were in the same room. When other members of the team had lunch together or chatted near the coffee machine, Keisha stayed at her desk, her gaze trained on her computer screen, typing furiously. She appeared withdrawn and anxious. Emily was curious about the change in attitude from one of her top team members, but she assumed that all would be revealed in the upcoming meeting.

And it was—but if anything, Emily was more mystified than ever.

Emily would *never* have expected that kind of question from Keisha. Since she'd started with the team, Keisha had been a confident go-getter whose ambition was backed up by her excellence and the quick pace at which she learned. In fact, she was so eager to take on extra responsibilities that, recently, Emily had started to notice Keisha's plate being a little over-filled. Nothing had slipped, but Keisha's workday had noticeably stretched over the past few months. She was almost always first at her desk in the morning, and many nights, Emily knew that it was Keisha who shut off the lights.

Emily recognized the subtle creep into overwork so well because it was a chronic tendency she herself shared. More than once, she'd caught herself getting completely wrapped up in the web of tasks and responsibilities that needed to be executed. She often had an overwhelming sense of obligation, keenly aware of her responsibility for her team's success. It sometimes felt that she was running on a hamster wheel of deadlines, trying to get ahead of a to-do list that never seemed to get shorter no matter how hard she attacked it—"done" was always on the horizon ahead of her, just out of reach.

As a result, she had a tendency to compromise on her personal boundaries, sacrificing self-time and home-time in service of her work.

Just another hour. I can pick up takeout on the way home.

I'll be able to knock out a few more hours at home if Jim helps Mackenzie with her homework tonight.

I'll put in a couple hours before the farmer's market on Sunday—I'll be able to clear my head if I do that.

If I switch gyms, I can get to work by 7:30 a.m. instead of 8:00.

It was the kind of slide that was difficult to see until she suddenly found herself with no free time, feeling less present with her kids, sleeping and eating badly, and feeling burned out. More than burned out, though, she also felt guilty.

Our sessions often focused on that guilt: "When I'm at home with my family, I feel guilty that everything at work is waiting for me," Emily would say. "But when I'm at work, I feel guilty that I'm not with my kids."

It compelled her into a cycle of overwork and a sense of not meeting the mark in any area of her life that she found tough to break.

Emily had lived this cycle a few times, and each time, she'd gotten better and better at recognizing it with the help of her own boss, Adrian.

Adrian had a great way of shutting down Emily's can't-turn-it-off work style in a way that still felt kind. He understood it was her default tendency to take on too much at times, so he'd quietly route work away from Emily until her task list became noticeably lighter and her stretched workday (that bled into nights and weekends) became harder to justify. Then he'd stop by Emily's office at 4:00 p.m. on a Friday with a twinkle in his eye.

"Time to go home. I know for a fact you don't have any more work keeping you here today. And before you make plans in your head to get more done, I want you to completely unplug this weekend. I'm going to be watching Slack—I'll know if you sign on."

That part was true. Emily had initially laughed it off, but the first time she'd disregarded Adrian's instructions and snuck online for some work on a Sunday afternoon—BAM, there he was, like her own personal stalker (but not the creepy kind).

Good afternoon, Emily! Respectfully, GET OFF SLACK and go relax with your family! See you tomorrow!

She may have grumbled, but she didn't need to be told twice; down went the lid of her laptop.

Despite the initial wash of frustration that came with her go-go-go work attitude being shut down, Emily also felt the glow of gratitude. Deep down, she felt cared for. Adrian was looking out for her because he valued her. He wanted her to feel her best, and he had her back when her subconscious overwork impulse—the devil on her shoulder—took the wheel.

In a lot of ways, it was the kind of care she'd never experienced in her life. Growing up as the oldest child of a single parent, she'd had to fend for herself a lot of the time. She'd always had a tendency toward perfectionism, and as a high-achieving adolescent, she often heard adults talk about how she could "do anything"—which made her feel like she needed to accomplish everything herself, without asking for help or support. Being self-sufficient and excelling on her own earned her praise, so it became her default mode. When she moved into adulthood, she defensively prided herself on not needing anyone to take care of her.

Secretly, she longed for someone to do just that. She worked harder than almost anyone else she knew. It would feel good for someone to take that burden off her shoulders once in a while so that she could just breathe.

So, when Keisha started showing the same signs of overwork, Emily had mentally rubbed her hands together in anticipation. *I know just how to solve this!* She was excited to show Keisha the same care Adrian had shown her so that Keisha could feel just as supported.

Emily had been quietly moving work off of Keisha's plate for the past few weeks. On one of Keisha's biggest projects, Emily had reassigned several large future milestones to other team members, keeping Keisha focused on big-picture direction as the project leader rather than in the weeds with execution.

If Keisha had noticed, she hadn't said anything. And actually, her conversations with Emily had dwindled of late. Despite Emily's efforts to support Keisha and lighten her load, Keisha seemed more stressed and chained to her desk than ever, and in meetings, she had gone from a confident, outspoken leader to a more reserved participant who often seemed anxious and unfocused.

Now Emily was face to face with a nervous, serious Keisha, who was apparently convinced she was in danger of being let go.

"Keisha, I don't know what to say—*what?* Why on earth would you think you were getting fired?"

Keisha frowned. "It's obvious that your confidence in my work has fallen. You've been taking work away from me for weeks. Did I do something wrong? It seems like you don't trust me to handle my plate anymore."

Oh.

Emily found herself flashing back to the summer of 2015, when her two kids had convinced her to do the Ice Bucket Challenge—the same ice-cold jolt of instant regret was washing through her.

Mentally, she slapped her forehead. *Well, that answers that!* She was now *crystal* clear on what was going on.

Later that week, Emily signed on for her coaching session with me. When her face appeared on my screen, she was wearing the most sheepish look I'd ever seen—I could tell she was about to tell me she'd messed up in some way.

"Yeah, so…turns out that Platinum Rule you've been drilling since day one?" she said, her voice dripping with irony. "Um…you were right. *It's a little important!*"

PEOPLE ARE THE POINT

As a leader, your job is to support, nourish, and empower the potential and performance of the people you lead.

For many of us who lead, we take that responsibility ultraseriously. Besides coffee, it's often the first thing we think about when we roll out of bed in the morning: *how can I bring out the absolute best in my team?*

For others of us, it feels more like the Sunday crossword, a puzzle we stare at for hours on end, unable to crack: *how can I possibly know what will motivate everyone best, and where would I find the time to discover that?*

Employees feeling valued is one of the top indicators of performance. In a survey from the American Psychological Association, among employees who report that they feel valued at work, 93 percent also report that they are motivated to do their best work, as opposed to just 33 percent of employees who say they don't feel valued.[4] Feeling valued also strongly correlates with employee engagement and satisfaction, and companies whose employees feel valued have strikingly lower turnover rates than companies whose employees feel unseen and unsupported.

Yet as leaders, when we're faced with a team member who needs our support, our instinctive reaction is to craft that support through the lens of what makes *us* feel supported. Our instinct is the Golden Rule—treating others how *we* want to be treated—when as leaders, we're better served by the Platinum Rule—treat others how *they* want to be treated.

The moment Keisha shared that she actually felt undervalued and incompetent as a result of Emily's actions, Emily realized she had been practicing gold, not platinum.

The way Adrian had supported Emily had felt so caring, so thoughtful. It had been so effective in helping Emily break out of an overwork spiral.

But Keisha didn't feel cared for. She didn't feel supported. She felt dismissed, pushed aside. She felt the trust she had once believed her boss had in her breaking.

By taking work off of Keisha's plate, Emily was saying, "I value you and don't want you to feel stressed and overwhelmed."

---

4 "APA Survey Finds Feeling Valued at Work Linked to Well-Being and Performance," American Psychological Association, 2012, https://www.apa.org/news/press/releases/2012/03/well-being.

Keisha heard, "I don't trust you to handle your workload. You're incompetent."

When I work with clients, stories like Emily's are some of the most common ones I hear. It's often bewildering how what we say could have been *heard* so differently from what we intended, and vice versa. All the smart tech in the world at our fingertips, and yet we might as well be talking to each other through tin can telephones.

I'll bet you've been right where Emily was at some point in your leadership career: trying to help someone on your team with all the best intentions, only to have those very efforts cause an even bigger disconnect.

Have you ever seen the famous physical comedy scene from *Frasier,* where Niles begins the scene sitting quietly by himself on the couch, and after an escalating series of mishaps and bungled attempts to fix them, he ends the scene passed out on the floor, pantsless, bleeding, and having set the couch on fire? It can feel like that sometimes—every move we make to fix the problem just makes a bigger mess.

We've all been there. As leaders, our instinct when we see a problem is to help.

But the way *you* see help isn't the way everyone else sees it.

In a way, Keisha bluntly asking if she was going to be fired was a huge gift for Emily. As leaders, it's not always so clear-cut how our communication is received. If what's heard by our team members is different from our intentions, we don't always know it right away. A low simmer of discontent can remain unseen for months or even years.

In order to truly help someone, you first have to discover how *they* see help. Only then can you craft the support they will be able to gratefully receive—the kind of support that will make them feel personally cared for.

This is the crux of the Platinum Rule: treat others how *they* want to be treated, not how *you* want to be treated.

UNDERSTAND SOMEBODY ELSE'S UNDERSTANDING

Let's rewind briefly to the moment I was talking about earlier, in grad school, when I first learned about the Platinum Rule.

I had come across the Platinum Rule early on in some of the pre-course reading I'd been doing. The specific wording came from the work of acclaimed communication researcher Milton Bennett. The deep reinforcement of the concept, however, came from the experience I had in my favorite class during my first semester in the program. It was a profoundly transformative moment, and its impact has been foundational to my career and relationships.

I remember this moment so clearly not just because of how much my mind was blown, but also because of the class itself, and the phenomenal professor who was teaching it: Dr. Eleanor Duckworth, a famous psychologist who studied under Piaget and was instrumental in groundbreaking pedagogy and curriculum development work in the 1960s.

Since I was in a self-designed master's program, I had been able to line up classes with all my academic heroes. In doing so, I was expected to contribute something original to their research during my time in their courses. It was nerve-racking, but thrilling. And the class I was by far the most eagerly anticipating was Dr. Duckworth's. As far as the world of psychology goes, Dr. Duckworth is a superstar. It was like taking a basketball lesson with Michael Jordan. I was totally starstruck.

The first day of class, butterflies in my stomach, I walked into the lecture hall and was immediately handed a journal by Dr. Duckworth's TA. I went to a seat in the front row and settled in as Dr. Duckworth began to take us through the syllabus.

Eventually, she got around to mentioning the journal we'd been handed. "In addition to your coursework," she began, and I swallowed—*in addition?* This was Harvard. The load wasn't exactly light. "…each night, I want you to look at the moon and capture what you see in this journal. You can draw a picture of it, write a poem about it—however you see it. The only requirement is that every single night, you capture something *new* about it."

I felt frustration settle across my shoulders like a wet blanket. *Draw? Poetry?* I was (and still am) incredibly artistically challenged. I didn't understand why she wanted us to draw the moon. And I knew my output would be…let's just say, *not* my best work.

The assignment was intimidating, and I was annoyed. But, clinging to my innate optimism, I told myself that there were exactly 105 nights coming up in the semester, and so I was going to nail the assignment in quantity at the very least.

Over the course of that fall and early winter, you could always tell a Duckworth student by the way we could be found wandering the campus at night staring up at the polluted Boston sky, trying to find the moon, then trying to write or draw anything about it in our identical journals. By the end of the semester, I had managed to capture all 105 nights of moons. My renderings ranged from vaguely interesting (one night I drew the reflection of the moon in a sidewalk puddle, the most artistic I have ever been and likely ever will be) to "what the heck *is that*" (any attempt at realism, and one misguided stab at a sonnet).

We turned in our journals the Friday before the last week of classes, and the following week, when we entered the lecture hall for our last class with Dr. Duckworth, the entire space was wallpapered edge to edge, floor to ceiling, with our moon captures. Thousands of journal pages, every surface completely covered.

Dr. Duckworth said to us, "Of everything you've learned in my class this term, what I want you to take away most is this. In just three months, we all captured *thousands* of ways to see the same object—the moon."

We all looked around in awe. The same flash of insight was clearly occurring to all of us: what we were seeing was the vast universe of human perspectives, all centered on the same unchanging object.

"Prior to this class, you might have assumed the moon could only be seen in one obvious way, and that everyone obviously sees it that way. But look around you. There are thousands of ways to see the moon, each one unique. Each one represents one person's understanding of the moon on one particular night. No two are the same."

Even just in the patch of wall right in front of where I stood, there were wildly divergent versions of the moon. The sheer difference from page to page was astounding.

"What I'm trying to teach you, and what I want you to take away from this class," Dr. Duckworth concluded, "is the idea of *understanding somebody else's understanding.*"

It was a famous saying of hers, one that I recognized from her writing. In that moment, everything clicked for me, like a flash of light—like a spark.

It had never occurred to me that there was more than one way to see the moon. That everyone didn't see it as I saw it.

But my classmates and I had managed to find a kaleidoscope of views of that same single object. We had come up with thousands of lenses to look through.

That day was when the Platinum Rule lodged itself in my head and set me on the course of what would become my career. The value of understanding somebody else's understanding was tremendous and crucial if I hope to understand *people,* and in doing so, leverage that understanding into more meaningful relationships.

Treat others as they want to be treated. I could only do that if I shattered my assumptions—which were based on my own perspective— and focused on discovering each individual's unique lens. Each new view of the moon was an opportunity for a new connection.

THE FALSE CONSENSUS EFFECT

Why do our minds so commonly default to our own perceptions and preferences?

Well, that's easy: the way we perceive the world is the only reference point we have. So our preferences and behavior are what we naturally assume others will share.

This phenomenon has a name: the *false-consensus effect*. When people are asked to guess how others will behave in a given situation, by and large, they vastly overestimate how many other people will share their beliefs, preferences, judgments, and reactions. More than that, they're often surprised when their perspective isn't shared. They assume that a different viewpoint must be rare.

It's like how people say, "*Everyone* knows that!" when something they believe is a fact is challenged. They're often surprised that, no, *not* everyone knows or even agrees, and the percentage who do know or agree is much, much lower than they assume.

The false-consensus effect is well known in certain workplaces; in fact, it comes up often in software teams when working on user experience design. The natural tendency is for designers to assume that if they find a particular workflow intuitive, most other people do, too.

These teams have a common saying to guard against this: *you are not the user.*

Social psychologist Brett Pelham writes:

> The need to belong (the desire to be accepted and connected to others) nudges people toward false-consensus effects. That is, we overestimate consensus for our own attitudes and behavior because we assume that other people who share our opinions are more likely to accept us. In a

sense, then, the false consensus effect is a form of wishful social thinking. It's reassuring to think that people agree with us.[5]

With all this in mind, it's no wonder that when trying to create moments of connection with the people we work with and lead—when reaching out a hand in service and support—we often rely on the only reference point we have: how *we* feel served and supported.

As a leader, your most powerful tool is the Platinum Rule. This one mindset shift is such a game changer, and so foundational to all the other methods we'll cover in this book, that it should be the first question you ask in any leadership situation.

How do they want to be treated?

If you don't know the answer, your job as a leader is to find out.

MINING FOR PLATINUM

Discovering how the people you lead want to be treated isn't as cut and dried as simply *asking* someone how they want to be treated (although that's not a bad place to start).

In the corporate world, most people have been conditioned that to speak up about their own wants and needs is to be selfish. The concept of "being a good team player" feeds into this; no one wants to be the one who draws an imbalance of attention to themselves (unless it's positive

---

5 Brett Pelham, "Your Opinions Are Not as Popular as You Think They Are: The False Consensus Effect," *Character and Context* (blog), Society for Personality and Social Psychology, October 25, 2019, https://www.spsp.org/news-center/blog/pelham-false-consensus.

attention, of course), the squeaky wheel causing friction. There's a fear of being labeled as "high maintenance" or "entitled." As a result, it's rare for employees to speak up about their needs when it comes to challenges around learning new things, receiving feedback on their work, or even maintaining their comfort and happiness.

Workplace Fulfillment in Numbers

The APA's 2012 study on workplace fulfillment[6] suggested a clear conclusion: employees who feel fulfilled are more engaged, more motivated, and more productive, and become advocates of the company to other high-potential employees.

- More than half of the employees who reported that they did not feel valued at work were planning to look for a new job in the next year.

- Respondents who reported feeling valued also reported feeling engaged and motivated to give their best.

- The feeling of value was correlated with better physical and mental health.

- Participants who felt undervalued measured the feeling based on being involved in decisions, advancement opportunity, pay strength, and non-monetary benefits like flex time to individually manage their work-life balance.

---

6 American Psychological Association, "APA Survey Finds Feeling Valued at Work."

As a result, leading by the Platinum Rule can sometimes feel like mining for platinum itself—an intensive process that involves digging in the deep darkness thousands of feet underground and using explosives to blow apart the rigid, packed-in ore.

But keep at it, and the return on that investment will be priceless.

Recently, Andy, a client of mine and the Chief People Officer at a rapidly scaling software company, was seeing a decline in the performance of new hires. He couldn't figure out why.

On a quarterly basis, he was responsible for running the onboarding of incoming "classes" of new team members, where they would learn everything they needed to know to be successful at the company.

"We have an incredibly in-depth onboarding process," he told me. "It's two weeks of focused learning. They see and learn everything about the business and the product they'll be working on before they take on a single task."

The problem was, the success rate out of the gate for new team members was a troubling 50 percent. Half of new team members consistently reported confusion and overwhelm, and needed time-intensive coaching, in the weeks and months following the onboarding.

"I don't get it," Andy said. "We put an incredible amount of work into our onboarding. It's as comprehensive as it can possibly be. We move through it really slowly and carefully, and we evaluate their understanding as we go. They *say* they get it. But once they actually get out on the floor, it's like they have no idea what they're doing. They respond as though we threw them in the deep end with no life jacket."

One day while we were troubleshooting, I asked him, more curiously than anything: "When you run these onboardings, how many of the new employees typically like to learn by doing, or by collaborating with other people, rather than watching and listening to a presentation?"

He blinked at me through the video chat. "What do you mean?"

"Well, you've said the onboarding is mostly PowerPoint presentations, with presenters leading lecture modules. That's going to be great for visual and auditory learners, but how many people in the room might be experiential or interpersonal learners?"

Andy was quiet for a moment, thinking. "You know," he said slowly, "I actually have no idea."

I could see the realization slowly dawn on him. He winced, then shook his head and laughed.

"*I've never asked.* It's never occurred to me. I've never even thought to ask them how they learn best!"

The next quarter, he came to our coaching call bubbling with triumph.

"Okay, so, it worked. This quarter's onboarding was amazing. The new hires are doing *great*—nine out of ten are crushing it and feel much more confident transitioning into their roles."

The only thing he'd changed? He started out the onboarding with a question for everyone: *How do you want to learn this material?*

He'd already prepared smaller breakout groups with leaders from the existing team, and once the new hires gave their answers—some preferred a visual walkthrough, some preferred a high-level presentation with a lot of talking and verbal processing, and some preferred to jump right in and "learn by doing"—it was simple enough to split into groups and teach people the way they wanted to be taught.

This simple shift not only improved the effectiveness of the onboarding but also welcomed the new hires to the team with an important implication: how they individually felt and perceived things was important, and would drive the actions of their leaders in this new workplace.

It can be more difficult to create this environment with people who are new to your leadership style and learning how to connect with you as their leader. They need time to build trust in you, and until they feel that trust, they're often cautious and reserved in volunteering their own needs. I hear people say all the time that they don't want to "come off as high-maintenance." They even take pride in their ability to "adapt to any situation."

That's just another way of saying that their needs have never been taken into account by their leaders—what they need has been *assumed*, not *known*.

And therein lies your greatest opportunity. You can show them a new way of leading, a way that forms deeper connections and greater empowerment than they've ever imagined was possible at work.

BUSINESS BREAKTHROUGHS

Employees who feel seen, understood, and valued as individuals are more likely to be motivated and engaged in their work—and committed to the organization. Companies with cultures built on individual recognition show employee engagement that's 2.5 times higher than companies where employees feel unseen and like "just a number," leading to higher productivity, greater retention, and a company culture that attracts the most talented candidates.[7]

IT BEGINS WITH YOU

In order to discover how the people you lead want to be treated, you'll begin by asking questions.

But not just any questions. This part takes some thought.

Remember that this is a little like platinum mining—the shiny stuff is buried deep. Simply asking, "What makes you feel fulfilled and valued at work?" is as likely to return actionable insight as blasting dynamite on the surface of the mine. You're not going to get in deep.

---

7   Caitlin Nobes, "9 Employee Engagement Statistics That Matter in 2021," Achievers, April 27, 2021, https://www.achievers.com/blog/employee-engagement-statistics/.

Instead, play detective. Craft questions that break apart the concept of "fulfilled" and "valued" and are easily understood, and just as easily answered. Questions like:

- What work makes you feel the most valuable to this team?

- What does a win look like to you? What does it feel like?

- If your ideal project landed on your desk tomorrow, what would it look like?

- What's one time you felt really supported by your team?

- What feels energizing to work on, and what feels draining?

- Is there anything that could be even better? What are your ideas on how to make that happen?

- If you were put in charge of this team tomorrow, what's the first thing you would change?

A team member whose wants and needs you're trying to discover might answer some of these questions like this:

I feel most valuable when I'm helping others solve a complicated technical problem.

A win for me looks like either a client or a teammate thanking me for helping them.

It feels really energizing to be in team meetings where we're collaborating and brainstorming, but it feels draining to knock through my admin tasks when they build up.

Right now, it's frustrating to see some of these new hires feel so clueless and lost.

If I were in charge, the first thing I'd do is assign each new hire a peer mentor so they can get more consistent attention from more perspectives.

If you read between the lines, these answers tell you clear as day what makes this person happy, and how they feel most fulfilled. Their brilliance is in collaboration, coaching, and service, especially using the expertise they've worked so hard for. They love to use that expertise to help people and groups solve problems. Furthermore, they likely want to be validated for their expertise and recognized for the service they provide to clients and teammates.

They want to be treated like a mentor and a collaborator.

With this information, you can tailor interactions you have with them to how *they want to be treated.* They'll feel seen, validated, and deeply fulfilled; their confidence and performance will skyrocket. Their brilliance will spread.

Most importantly, their trust in you as their leader will be strengthened exponentially. They'll be more likely to open up to you about what they need in the future—which means you, as their leader, will be able to do your job that much better.

This isn't where your job ends, though.

Recall Lauren's predicament from the Introduction. Lauren had led her team into a set of mindsets and behaviors not through any intentional steps; they had followed the lead she had modeled for them.

You're the sparkler that lights all the other sparklers. The mindsets and behaviors you want to see in your team begin with you.

Do *you* know how you want to be treated?

If you're reading this and you immediately said *of course!* in your mind, stop. Take a moment to reflect on the question.

Do you *really* know how you want to be treated?

As leaders, we're so often focused on the people we serve that any focus on ourselves often falls by the wayside. Of all the hundreds of clients I've coached in Platinum Leadership, the percentage who had taken the time to truly think about and understand how they wanted to be treated before we began our work together is remarkably small.

If this surprises you, remember the false-consensus effect. *Everyone knows how they want to be treated! Right?*

In my experience, *wrong.*

Platinum Leadership begins with you. The same questions that you craft to mine the platinum deep within each member of your team are the same questions you'll begin by asking yourself.

In that spirit, before we move on to the next chapter, here's a self-evaluation and some next steps to take with your team that will set you on your path.

YOU GET SOLID: SELF-EVALUATION

1. When do you feel most valuable as a leader?

2. What does a win look and feel like to you?

3. How do you feel most supported?

4. What work feels energizing to you? What work drains your energy?

5. What, if anything, is frustrating you in your leadership right now?

6. What aspects of your leadership could be even better? What are your ideas on how to make that happen?

7. What feedback from your team would make you feel most validated in your leadership?

THEY GET SOLID: NEXT STEPS

1. Give the same self-evaluation to your team members, and review the responses at an informal roundtable.

2. Make it a practice to check in with these questions at a regular cadence. This will ensure your interactions are evolving and growing alongside people, their roles, and their needs.

2

UNDERSTAND

One thousand employees surveyed by Harris/Interact said that the number one critical skill lacked by 91 percent of leaders is "communicating well."[8]

"We have to lay people off."

Dominic, the owner of a growing fintech company, had barely gotten the words out of his mouth when his cofounder, Max, interrupted. The Zoom line had a brief burst of static as the two electronic voices fought for dominance.

"We've been through hard times before! We just added a hundred people this year, and they're all necessary. We can figure this out, but we *can't* lose anyone."

"You can't fill a flat tire that still has a leak!" argued Dominic. "It's impossible."

---

8   Marcel Schwantes, "Survey: 91 Percent of 1,000 Employees Say Their Bosses Lack This 1 Critical Skill," *Inc.*, August 10, 2017, https://www.inc.com/marcel-schwantes/survey-91-percent-of-1000-employees-say-their-boss.html.

Max was aghast. "What would be *impossible* is expecting us to keep growing without the people we need to get the work done!"

"No. We have to figure out a plan to lay people off."

"*No*. We have to figure out a plan to *make more money* so we don't have to lay anyone off."

Back and forth, back and forth.

It wasn't the first time a coaching session with two of my favorite clients, this pair of former big-corporate coworkers who had struck out on their own together, had devolved into chaos. In fact, Dominic and Max had so many in-session arguments that I'd asked them weeks ago to call in separately to the Zoom line—simply so that they were forced to let each other talk (and so that I had the power to mute them if they wouldn't).

When Dominic and Max had started their business together, they'd enjoyed a year-long honeymoon. As coworkers at their old company, they'd always been each other's sounding board; as business partners, their vastly different personalities served as a complementary glue that knit them together. They were each other's wingman, other half, devil's advocate.

But over time, those differences had begun to act more like speedbumps. The critical need to make decisions together on the regular as cofounders, not just friends, had proved difficult.

Actually, that's an understatement. Agreeing on *anything* about the business was difficult for them.

Their perspectives couldn't have been more opposite. And now, as their business had come up on the first real "money troubles" of its young life, they were close to civil war—close enough that they'd each already dug out their trenches in anticipation of the fight.

Dominic, the company's financial mind, head accountant, CFO, and the more cerebral and pessimistic of the two, was playing defense, declaring they needed to hand out pink slips ASAP or their business was going down.

Max, the more outgoing, optimistic, and leadership-oriented of the pair, was playing offense, positive a few more points could even things up but uncertain of the score.

At that moment, talking it out wasn't helping. The more they talked, the less they heard. Like so many other calls I'd been on with Dominic and Max, the communication breakdown was making forward momentum nearly impossible.

We were going to have to try something else, and *fast*.

ALL AROUND US, ALL THE TIME

The late, great American writer David Foster Wallace opened his now-famous 2005 commencement speech to the graduating class at Kenyon College with the following anecdote:

> There are these two young fish swimming along and they happen to meet an older fish swimming the other way, who nods at them and says "Morning, boys. How's the water?" And the two young fish swim on for

a bit, and then eventually one of them looks over at the other and goes "What the hell is water?"[9]

This is how I often think about the concept of interpersonal communication. It's something we all do so constantly, so naturally, that we really don't think about *how* we're doing it.

Have you ever driven to work or the grocery store and realized you had no memory of how you got there? All the turns you took, lanes you crossed, decisions you made to stop or go or merge or check your blind spot... they were so automatic, they disappeared. Yet because of them, and *only* because of them, you arrived.

For leaders, communication is like this—as easy to overlook as it is vital. Because if you don't do it right, you and your team end up at the wrong destination or, sometimes worse, going around in circles. Remember the Griswolds in *European Vacation* stuck driving in the roundabout, and all Clark Griswold can do is point out, "Look, kids...Big Ben...Parliament!" over and over as they make circles till nightfall? Total frustration. No one wants that.

Guess where we start? Connection is impossible without fluid, clear, and mutually understood communication—so it's no coincidence that when I begin working with clients, the first thing we focus on is communication. It's often the most immediate, and highest, wall between them and the people they work with (And don't worry—we dive into connection in an upcoming chapter).

---

9 David Foster Wallace, "This Is Water" (speech), 2005 Commencement Address, Kenyon College, Gambier, Ohio, http://bulletin-archive.kenyon.edu/x4280.html.

I just had a really tough conversation, and I don't think it went well.

I just gave someone on my team feedback, and they reacted terribly. They got so defensive; they shut down.

The common thread in these concerns is uncertainty. They have a gut feeling that the communication was off. But they're not sure why.

They'll say, "I just don't know if they truly understood what I meant."

My response is simple: "Did you ask?"

Usually, they'll pause for a moment with a quizzical expression before answering with a question of their own: "Duh—why didn't I think of that?"

It's a forehead-smack moment, and yet it's so often overlooked—if you want to know how someone is hearing or receiving you, the best way to know for sure is to ask. In fact, I recommend whenever you're working with someone new to start with questions specifically about communication. You could ask:

- How do you prefer to hear feedback? (Written or verbally? In the moment, or later on?)

- Can you think of a conversation you had with a previous coworker or boss that didn't go well for you? What made it not feel good?

- Can you share a time when a tough conversation went well, and what part of it felt good to you?

- How frequently do you like to meet?

These questions establish the baseline of how you want to interact with one another. What a great way to begin to build communication *and* connection.

CONNECTION PROBLEMS...OR COMMUNICATION PROBLEMS?

"It's just difficult to get through to him sometimes—you know, because of our dynamic."

Dynamic was the code word Joe, a marketing executive at a midsize financial planning company, had come up with to describe how he felt about working with Nolan, another member of the executive team. I'd become accustomed to him dropping the phrase as a more positive version of the truth (for which I gave him credit).

The truth being that, from Joe's perspective, they were at each other's throats.

Nolan, the company's VP of Product, couldn't have been more opposite from Joe in personality, leadership style, and energy. When Nolan walked into the room, he filled it entirely. He naturally projected his voice and spoke up often—usually with the clearest voice at the table. That wasn't to say Nolan was an interrupter, or didn't let others speak; he was a good listener and led the way in asking for all perspectives during a group discussion. It was more that his communication style— self-assured, confident, with an obvious conviction in his opinions— belied a clear belief that when it came time for a decision, it would be *his* decision, even if it was the CEO who technically made the final call.

And most of the time, it *was* Nolan's decision. Joe had no problem giving credit where credit was due. Nolan, he acknowledged, was an excellent leader whose hit rate on decisions was near perfect. He had all the makings of the company's next CEO: a decision engine who knew how to listen to all perspectives, analyze the available information, and ultimately call the right play.

Joe, in contrast, had a calm, level energy, a thoughtful presence, and processed information best on his own. He was a methodical problem solver who liked to make sure he'd overturned every stone before deciding the best course of action.

His more careful, paced leadership style made a great counterbalance to Nolan. On the big, meaty issues their team dealt with—decisions like hiring and firing, product development, and company vision and direction—their CEO often commented that he wanted Joe to take his time and come back to him with his deeply considered insights before the team made a call. "There's no decision this team can't sleep on," their CEO often said.

Joe's problem wasn't that he felt edged out by Nolan. He was assured of his own role and impact in the company.

His problem was that when the issue *wasn't* big and meaty, by the time it came up for discussion, Nolan would already have made his own decision *and* taken action. The CEO was delighted by the quick movement and greenlit nearly every single one.

The game was over before Joe even got on the field.

"And don't get me wrong; his decisions are good. He's a great thinker and problem solver. So our CEO considers the issue dealt with, and the team moves on to the next fire we need to put out," Joe told me.

Joe had spoken up before in executive team meetings about considering alternate perspectives. He'd even pointed out in those meetings that it would be great for team members to sleep on it—using the CEO's own catch-phrase—think through solutions, and then regroup. From his perspective, it was less about the decision itself, and more about giving everyone time and space to participate in the thinking process.

The CEO liked to move fast. His decision-making style was typically more in line with Nolan's unless it was a major decision with lots of implications. In fact, he often described Nolan as "a younger version of myself."

Joe was secure in being himself, with his own style. But he felt like he was stuck on the bench.

Over the months I'd been coaching both Joe and Nolan, Joe's unease had built into resentment. He felt like he was stagnating in his growth simply because he had a different thinking and communication style than the star player, who seemed like the CEO's clear favorite.

"I have no attachment to being the favorite," Joe said. "And I know I'm not in the running for CEO. I'm carving my own career and leadership path. But right now, I have no chance to shine. I can't get my foot in the door because Nolan *always* beats me to it."

He'd tried talking to Nolan about it. Nolan had, in Joe's opinion, dismissed the conversation.

So now Joe's resentment had a clear face and name: a Johnny Lawrence–esque nemesis named Nolan.

"Can you describe the 'dynamic' between you that you're referring to?" I asked Joe on one of our calls. "I want to make sure I understand where you see the communication breaking down."

"We just butt heads. We have such different styles and opinions that whenever I bring an idea to him, it either gets dismissed immediately as something he 'already decided against,' or he looks at me like I have two heads."

On my next coaching session with Nolan, I decided to check out the other side of the coin.

"Can I ask about your working relationship with Joe? How would you characterize it?" I asked.

Nolan's face stayed calm and positive. If he felt any flash of negative emotion, he didn't show it.

"I'd characterize it as good, but definitely distant," he replied. "Sometimes I feel like we're not always speaking the same language. But I really value his energy and insights, and he has great ideas. It's a good relationship."

I pressed a little more, and asked him about, in Joe's words, their "dynamic."

Now Nolan looked confused. "What dynamic?"

It was clear to me that Nolan had no idea what I was talking about.

They didn't have a *connection* problem—they had a *communication* problem. And that was great news (it's fixable!).

Many people think effective communication is saying what you want to say. It's one of those things that sounds like it should be true, yet it's not.

Communication is only effective when the message is received *accurately*.

That's what I said! Who hasn't frustratedly defended themselves this way once or twice to a child, spouse, or coworker? Or at least wanted to? (Guilty.)

As a leader, you're focused on how your team members want to be treated— how they perceive, receive, and process input. With that in mind, it doesn't matter what you *said*. What matters is how what you said was *received*—if it was received at all. Focus on that, and you'll build a team with wonderful communication, stellar connection, and incredible results.

In workplaces with great communication culture, team members and leaders are on the same page, and so is everyone involved. The vision is clear, expectations are even clearer, and discussions don't end until everyone is sure what they're supposed to do next. The positive effects on the business are stunning; companies that communicate effectively are more than *four times* more likely to retain the best employees.

And yet communication between leaders and teams, and between workplace peers, is one of the top challenges faced by any organization. Sixty-nine percent of managers report being "not comfortable" communicating with their employees[10]—which dovetails clearly with the fact that 1000 employees surveyed by Harris/Interact said that the number one critical skill lacked by 91 percent of leaders is "communicating well."[11]

---

10 Lou Solomon, "Two-Thirds of Managers Are Uncomfortable Communicating with Employees," *Harvard Business Review*, March 9, 2016, https://hbr.org/2016/03/two-thirds-of-managers-are-uncomfortable-communicating-with-employees.

11 Schwantes, "Survey: 91 Percent of 1,000 Employees."

Fifty-seven percent of employees report not being clear on what they're supposed to be doing.[12] They're not very happy, either—33 percent of employees said that a lack of open, honest communication has the greatest negative impact on their morale.[13]

A recent Interact/Harris poll dived deep into the specifics of what poor communication between leaders and employees looks like. These were the factors that showed up most commonly on employees' lists:[14]

- Not recognizing employee achievements (63 percent)

- Not giving clear directions (57 percent)

- Not having time to meet with employees (52 percent)

- Refusing to talk to subordinates (51 percent)

- Taking credit for others' ideas (47 percent)

- Not offering constructive criticism (39 percent)

- Not knowing employees' names (36 percent)

- Refusing to talk to people on the phone/in person (34 percent)

- Not asking about employees' lives outside of work (23 percent)

---

12 Solomon, "Two-Thirds of Managers Are Uncomfortable."

13 Michael Gadd, "Poor Communication Hurts Morale," *Inc.*, November 6, 2008, https://www.inc.com/news/articles/2008/11/communication.html.

14 Schwantes, "Survey: 91 Percent of 1,000 Employees."

Communication in Numbers

- According to a McKinsey report, well-connected teams with great communication see a productivity increase of 20-25 percent.[15]

- Ninety-seven percent of employees believe communication impacts how efficient they are on a daily basis.[16]

- Employees working in organizations with effective communication plans—ones that manage to minimize the silo effect and centralize communication—are 3.5 times more likely to outperform their peers.[17]

- Eighty percent of Americans believe employee communication is crucial for developing trust with employers.[18]

---

15   Michael Chui, et al., "The Social Economy: Unlocking Value and Productivity Through Social Technologies," McKinsey Global Institute, July 1, 2012, https://www.mckinsey.com/industries/technology-media-and-telecommunications/our-insights/the-social-economy.

16   Lori Alcala, "4 Trends in Workplace Communication," CMSWire, January 20, 2015, https://www.cmswire.com/cms/social-business/4-trends-in-workplace-communication-infographic-027762.php.

17   John French, "Towers Watson Research Study on Effective Communication and ROI," Bizcommunity.com, March 10, 2014, https://www.bizcommunity.com/Article/196/500/110632.html.

18   "9 Statistics That Prove You Need Internal Communications," Lexicon (via SlideShare), July 28, 2016, https://www.slideshare.net/LexiconDSM/9-statistics-that-prove-you-need-internal-communications.

> • A study by Salesforce that included not only employees but corporate executives and educators as well shows that 86 percent believe ineffective communication is the underlying reason for workplace failures.[19]

GROUND RULES FOR GREAT COMMUNICATION

Your leadership begins with communication. Great communication requires attention, intention, and practice.

Action #1: Assume the Best of Intentions

You're going to be well served entering into *any* interaction by assuming positive intent. Conversely, assuming ill intent can harm your leadership in the long run by eroding the trust you've built with your team members.

Picture it: you've just been dressed down by a client who's irate over a mistake made by your team. It's a mistake they've made before, and you've coached them on it, but it's still cropped up again like a weed.

You go into the next team meeting, guns blazing, ready to be firm with your expectations—*this can't happen again.* After laying out the problem for your team, you notice they're frowning, not nodding sheepishly. They look annoyed, not receptive.

---

19 "How Soft Skills Are Crucial to Your Business," Salesforce Canada, August 20, 2014, https://www.salesforce.com/ca/blog/2014/08/how-soft-skills-are-crucial-to-your-business-.html.

You later find out that the mistake the client ranted to you about? That wasn't the team's mistake at all. In fact, the team had repeatedly set expectations for the client about what would happen if the client didn't listen to their advice on the project. The client made their choice, the project floundered, and the client's response was to call you up and blame it on your team.

And you believed the client. Immediately. Without reminding yourself that your team operates with the best of intentions, and asking yourself if you might not be getting the full story.

If you don't assume your fellow team members are acting with the best intentions, it can come at the price of a loss of trust, and even otherwise harmless or well-intentioned conversations can develop an emotional charge. When you give your coworkers the benefit of the doubt by assuming the best of intentions, conversations immediately become much easier and far less complicated.

Action #2: Be Curious

When you assume the best of intentions, you avoid defensiveness and distrust, and are freed up to communicate, instead, with curiosity. You can ask questions without jumping to conclusions, minimizing someone else's idea, or getting defensive. You can understand their perspective much better.

I've coached dozens of leaders through defensiveness that often arises when they're confronted with a challenging question. Because most leaders have worked hard to achieve their position and have a high degree of confidence in their decisions, a simple question can often feel like a rebuke. *Don't you trust me? Why do I have to explain my decisions? Haven't I shown that I won't steer us wrong?*

Let's reframe this situation through Action #1. If we assume the best of intentions, a challenging question about a decision you've made is just that—a question. Someone isn't clear on the *why* behind the decision, so they're curiously seeking to understand.

With this frame, you can respond with curiosity in kind. *Tell me more about what's not clear to you. Can you be more specific? I want to make sure I understand what you're looking to know.*

Understandably, people become defensive when they feel like they're being unfairly criticized. But if you combine assuming the best of intentions and interacting with others from a place of curiosity, even emotionally charged situations can be quickly diffused.

Picture yourself in an argument with your husband. You spend an hour painstakingly laying out all the wrongs you've perceived, *very clearly*, and at the end, he looks at you blankly.

"I still don't get why you're mad," he says.

Steam shoots out of your ears *Looney Tunes*–style, and you take the deepest breath of your life, because you're about to *explode.*

Imagine if instead, he responded with, "Can you tell me more about why you're feeling this way? I want to understand."

No shouting match, no bad vibes for the rest of the night—he's curiously seeking to understand, and you know he cares about how you feel. There's connection there, where before there was only anger.

When people are defensive, there's very little chance of a productive outcome. But when you're curious, there's always an opening for one.

"I just want you to be happy…"

You've undoubtedly heard this before from someone in your life: "I just want you to be happy."

Our parents say it to us. We say it to our spouses and our kids. We want it for our team. But in my experience, I rarely hear anyone ask—from a Platinum perspective—the *obvious* next question: "What does happy mean to you?"

When I run up against a concept I'm curious about, diving deep into research is *my* happy place. Earlier in my career, I did a study where I asked 800 children, ages kindergarten to sixth grade, a question:

"What does happy mean to you?"

They could write or draw their answer, or both. The variety in the responses was striking. Some—many—were hilarious. One was: "Happy to me is playing video games with a group of friends and laughing together and telling private jokes." Another kid wrote:

"Happy to me is playing games by myself on my bed and my bed is made of gold."

Often, what we do to create happiness for other people is based on our own assumptions. Looking at these two children, I never would have known how radically different their ideas of happiness were.

Whenever I'm wondering something about someone or something, when I don't feel clear but I *think* I have an idea, I remember that fourth grader and his bed of gold. And I realize something: I actually don't know. I don't know at all. Luckily, though, I can almost always find out—by showing curiosity, and by listening to understand.

Action #3: Listen to Understand

This is the counterpart to Be Curious. Asking questions is überimportant—but how you listen is just as crucial.

The next time someone tells you what they think or how they feel, notice:

Are you listening to *understand?*

Or are you listening to decide if you agree or disagree?

Perhaps you're not really listening at all—you're internally formulating what you're going to say next?

If you can relate, hello and welcome; we've all been there. We listen to respond nearly automatically, and not because we're rude. Typically, it's because we're excited—we want to build on their comment, or it sparked a memory or new idea we want to share.

Listening to understand requires taking yourself out of the equation and focusing entirely on the other person. What they're saying is not about *you*. It's about them—what they think, what they feel, what they need.

So, pause. Digest what they're saying. You can tell you're listening to understand when every word the other person says inspires a new opportunity to understand them more deeply. Questions come to you that will help you connect; you're intrigued and driven to fully understand what they're communicating to you.

Asking follow-up questions that take the conversation deeper—and importantly, that keep it focused on *them*—lets the other person know that they're being truly heard. And when you're listening to understand, you might find that you need time to sit with their message before continuing the conversation. There's no rush to respond; understanding takes time.

Action #4: Use "I" Statements

What I hear you saying is...

From what I understand, you'd like to...

In communication, the only thing you know for sure is what you received. By communicating this using "I" statements like the above, you leave the assumptions off the table, out of the debate. You are owning your perspective.

"I" statements signal an openness that's critical to good communication. By using them, you show you understand that your perspective might be different from someone else's. Communicating what you received moves the conversation forward and eliminates confusion. Often, following up "I" statements with a question—"Is that right?" or "Am I understanding this correctly?"—can help, too.

Action #5: Infuse Positivity

Remember that the team's mood and outlook begin with you. And communicating an uplifting outlook at work has incredible individual and collective business results, according to the *Harvard Business Review*. It:

- Increases sales by 37 percent.

- Raises productivity by 31 percent.

- Boosts profits by 50 percent.

- Decreases the negative effects of stress by 23 percent.

Positive Psychology researcher Michelle Gielan asserts that the best time to infuse positivity is when you begin conversations. She calls this a Power Lead. "Nowhere is your power to meaningfully influence others more evident than at the start of an interaction," writes Michelle. "The way we start off conversations, meetings, emails, and phone calls often predicts how they unfold."[20]

When starting a conversation, Slack message, or email with your team, be optimistic. Think about something that was fun or brought you joy, and share it. It will set the tone for the entire conversation—and positively impact the resulting thinking, perspectives, and outcomes.

Recently, I had a busy day of meetings and the thought of what to make for dinner, once again, had taken a backseat. So, feeling a bit bedraggled after scooping up the boys from their after-school activities, I hit the In-N-Out drive-thru. Our cashier, Madison (I'll never forget her name!), glanced curiously at the two boys in the backseat. As she handed me our delicious-smelling paper bags full of food, she mentioned offhand, "Wow, you look too young to have two kids that age!"

I melted. "I was not expecting that, and you have no idea how much I needed that! You made my night!" I gushed. Madison smiled hesitantly and shrunk back slightly into the drive-thru window, clearly wondering what can of worms she'd accidentally opened with this harried, messy-ponytailed, emotionally unstable customer. Meanwhile, I drove off on cloud nine.

The next morning, I told a group I was working with about Madison's comment. I asked how their previous nights had gone. Sure enough, almost everyone shared a positive story, and we had one of our most productive, energetic sessions ever.

---

20 Michelle Gielan, "Power Lead Your Next Conversation," BetterUp, September 2, 2019, https://www.betterup.com/blog/power-lead-your-next-conversation.

BUSINESS BREAKTHROUGHS

When you create a curious communication culture—when all team members assume the best intentions, approach situations with curiosity, listen to understand, and are in the habit of showing up with positivity—it has a direct measurable ROI. Companies with great communicators report returns to shareholders 47 percent higher than companies that suffer in communication skills.[21]

IS EVERYONE BEING HEARD?

Joe wasn't the only team member who'd shared with me that Nolan tended to take up all the space in every conversation he was a part of.

In fact, I'd heard it from no less than three other employees at the organization—two of them Nolan's direct reports, and one of them the leader of another team.

Each person who brought it up said some version of the same thing: "There's no space to speak up when he's in the room. It's like the conversation goes in the direction he takes it, with no opportunity for anyone else to drive—and he thinks and moves so quickly that it feels impossible to keep up sometimes."

---

21 Robert Sher, "Never Leave Internal Communications to Chance in Midsized Companies," *Forbes*, July 17, 2014, https://www.forbes.com/sites/robertsher/2014/07/17/never-leave-internal-communications-to-chance-in-midsized-companies/?sh=7d3c17316c6a.

This is, without a doubt, one of the most common traits I notice in the people I coach. And it makes sense; leaders who have achieved high levels of success usually didn't get there by accident. They got there by being smart, effective, outspoken, and driving the conversation.

Not everyone wants, or is cut out, to be a leader—and some who are just haven't gotten there yet.

But that doesn't mean that only leaders want to *speak*.

To create a team culture built on great communication, all voices need space to be heard. Sure, each person has a responsibility to speak up. But take a moment to think about the environment you foster in the team you lead—are you making space for all those different voices?

Or are a few of the loudest ones taking up all the space?

Amplifying all voices is active, not passive. Instead of leaving it to each person to speak up, actively create opportunities for all voices. Ask the quieter members of the team what they think. In front of everyone, bring up the insights a more gun-shy team member shared with you. Or just sit with the silence; often, the best nuggets of wisdom and connection lie in the moments of silence between the talking.

A great communication culture is one where every person on a team is secure in the value of their contributions, and is certain that their leader wants to hear and understand them. If you build it, they will speak.

Nolan, like Joe had acknowledged many times, had great strength as a listener.

When I coached Nolan to understand the aspects of his personality and manner that were causing disconnects with so many members of the team, he listened to understand. And he heard me.

The next time I hopped on a session with Joe, he had a grin on his face and eyed me suspiciously. "You said something, didn't you?"

He told me that the executive team had just come from their quarterly planning retreat, a two-day event that tackled a massive agenda of hot-button issues. The big ones, as usual, the team all discussed together, and the CEO mandated that they sleep on it.

When the smaller decisions came up, Joe braced himself for the usual rapid-fire rapport between Nolan and the CEO—and for his own ideas to sit unheard.

But where Nolan would usually jump in enthusiastically with thoughts and a plan of action, he sat back and looked at his teammates.

"I have some ideas," he said, and gave a self-deprecating wink, "*of course.* But this is an area where I'd like to hear what Joe thinks, actually."

The room turned to Joe, all eyes on him.

It was his moment, and he grabbed the opportunity.

That one moment, he told me later, completely broke open the invisible stranglehold Nolan had had on the conversation. More and more, other team members spoke up. Each time a new issue was raised, Nolan either sat quietly waiting for others to have their say first, or asked specific people for their opinions. He asked follow-up questions and listened intently, approaching each idea with curiosity.

In the end, the decisions that were made were, Joe said, almost certainly *exactly* what Nolan would have decided in the first place. But by creating space for everyone else to take part in the decision-making, the connection throughout the team got noticeably stronger as the days went on, and buy-in on the decisions was at an all-time high.

COMMUNICATION = CONNECTION = SUCCESS

Back to Dominic and Max, my own personal real-life reenactment of *Captain America: Civil War.* (But with slightly less hand-to-hand combat.)

I knew I needed to hear out Dominic and Max separately so I could understand their thoughts clearly. I met with Max first.

"I really don't want to lay people off," he told me, empathetic and optimistic as always. "I need to know if there's a way we can financially make this work."

As I asked more questions, it occurred to me Max didn't just want to avoid layoffs; he wanted *data.* "I'm curious how much money we need and how many clients we need to bring on to make it happen," he said.

Huh. I think I know someone who knows a thing or two about data.

I talked to Dominic. His frustration was obvious, and the communication breakdown with his partner and best friend was making his natural pessimism overwhelm his thinking.

"Max keeps saying, 'Oh, we're great. This will pass,'" says Dominic. "*We're not great!* We need to make a huge amount of money to keep our people...it's basically impossible."

"How much exactly?" I asked.

Dominic paused; I'd disrupted his gloom train. "What do you mean?"

"You're the numbers guy. You can probably rattle off the cash flow forecast off the top of your head," I said. "You keep saying it would take a huge amount of money to avoid layoffs. What's that dollar amount?"

(If you've never watched an accountant whip through complex calculations in their head, try to find an opportunity. It's fascinating.)

"Two million," Dominic said after about ten seconds. "Two million. See? It's insane."

And there it was. The data Max needed, the score, the amount they both wanted to recoup. I could see they were on the same side and wanted to do exactly the same thing—pull the company through the rough spot and continue to grow. But they were too busy defending their positions to actually talk facts.

Next, I scheduled a session with the three of us. I'd discussed with each of them previously that I wanted to begin with them acknowledging each other's strengths.

Max told Dominic that he appreciated his methodical, analytical role in their business, and how essential his grounded realism was.

Dominic told Max that they likely wouldn't even have started the company, let alone taken it as far as they had, without his optimism and ability to close big deals.

"Well, on that note," Max said, "can you show me how much we're missing? I can look at our potential pipeline and see what I can do. What's the exact dollar amount, and how much time do I have?"

The goal to avoid layoffs was suddenly about hard numbers—Dominic's happy place. "We probably have a good three months with our reserves," Dominic said cautiously. "But we need to bring in two million in new business."

"Got it," Max said. "Now it's time to get to work."

By curiously asking questions and listening to understand, they had realized they weren't competitors, but teammates.

They began talking through strategies for bringing in the two million. Ideas were introduced and dismissed, some gained traction, and some were instant winners. Then Dominic offhandedly mentioned a memory of one of their first pitch sessions from when they had started the company.

"That's it," Max said.

"What's it? That pitch won't work again."

"No, *us pitching together.* Remember that?" said Max. "You had the data, and I had the ideas. It was like peanut butter and jelly. People loved it! What if…what if you go on these pitches with me? We have a better shot of closing if we go in as a team."

Dominic smiled. I could tell that, for the first time in a long time, the partners were on the same page; the civil war was over, and now they could move forward united.

YOU GET SOLID: SELF-EVALUATION

1. When's the last time you felt you weren't being heard? Can you pinpoint why you felt that way?

2. Think back to the last conversation you had with a team member that felt like it had friction. What are three questions you could have asked in order to curiously discover where they were coming from?

3. Consider each member of your team. Are you certain they're all being equally heard? If not, brainstorm some ways you can bring the quieter voices to the front.

THEY GET SOLID: NEXT STEPS

1. Ask your team members: "How do you prefer to receive feedback?" Document each person's answer to create a feedback guide for the whole team.

2. Hold a mini-workshop with your team that establishes the ground rules for great communication and gives opportunities to practice.

3

ALIGN

According to a Franklin Covey survey, 55 percent of employees report that they don't know what their organization's mission and purpose are.[22]

In fact, only one in seven employees can name a current company goal.

Six out of seven employees are flying blind when it comes to the expectations of their leadership.

My husband Rob began his career at age fifteen cleaning cars in the detailing center of a local car dealership. It was his first job, and to this day, it's the only job he's ever been fired from.

When he tells the story about why he got fired, he paints a dramatic picture, a villainous caricature of an inept, out-of-touch manager versus a rebellious but pure-hearted teenager. There's definitely some embellishment. But it's one of my favorite stories about employee-manager

---

22 "Clarifying Your Team's Purpose and Strategy," FranklinCovey survey, *Leadership Modular Series*, 2016, https://franklincovey.ro/wp-content/uploads/2016/12/MODULE-CLARIFY-ING-YOUR-TEAMS-PURPOSE-AND-STRATEGY-clarifying_purpose-pdf.pdf.

miscommunication, because it so perfectly illustrates the subject of this chapter: why, as a leader practicing the Platinum Rule, your very first job is to make *absolutely sure* that you and your team members are 100 percent aligned on expectations.

Without this alignment, it doesn't matter how well everyone connects, grows, and performs—the success of your team, and your company, is at risk right out of the gate.

Rob was a sophomore in high school and just looking to make a little spending money when he applied at the local Nissan dealership. Back then, the primary role of a car detailer was sealant removal. All the newly shipped-in cars came covered with a sealant (almost certainly chock-full of asbestos) that had to be scrubbed off with a nostril-burning solvent. When Rob was handed a bucket of toxic chemicals and an array of detailing tools from handheld vacuums to Q-tips, and told to contort his body into various back-breaking yoga-like positions to get into every tiny crevice of the cars, he figured that was par for the course and happily went to work.

The only problem was his manager, Ted, a man whom Rob describes as "ninety-seven on a young day" (from a teenager's POV—so, not a day over forty). Ted would walk back and forth across the line of new cars being scrubbed, squinting disapprovingly at every move of their Q-tips, his brow furrowed. There was no escaping his eye; it was like working in a fishbowl.

At the end of Rob's first day, his hands stinging slightly and his clothes radiating carcinogens, Ted's feedback was curt: "Do better."

Do better? That was it? *Okay,* Rob thought, *I must have missed a few spots.* The next day, he triple-checked every inch of the car he worked on, running his hand over the glossy surface to feel for the slightest trace of dust or sealant. He was satisfied that it was perfect.

Ted, at the end of the day: "No, this needs to be better. You're not doing it right."

Now, of course, any of us as adults given such feedback would have done the natural thing and asked for clarification. "What does 'better' mean?" or "What should I do differently?"

Fifteen-year-old Rob, naive, annoyed, and with a budding anti-authoritarian streak he would later pass on to our older son (thanks, honey), did not ask questions. Instead, he stubbornly tried every form of "better" he could think of. He brought in old t-shirts of increasing softness to shine the chrome. He got more obsessive with the Q-tips until they were the primary tool in his arsenal. He wore out his tape of *The Karate Kid* studying "wax on, wax off." No matter what he did, Ted the manager hovered just over his shoulder at all times.

This went on for two weeks. Ted frowned and shook his head at Rob's work every day, and Rob got more and more desperate with his attempts to "do better."

Eventually, the inevitable happened. "This isn't for you, son," Rob's manager said to him on his second Friday. "Today's your last day. Here's your check."

As Rob tells it, he proceeded to reenact the famous quitting scene from *Half Baked* while his coworkers clapped and cheered him out the door. (The fact that *Half Baked* wouldn't be made for another ten years when Rob was fifteen somehow doesn't put him off that triumphant flourish.)

Now, you may be thinking, *Well, sure, but that manager was horrible. A good leader would know how to communicate exactly what they want from their employees.*

In my experience, though, misalignment on expectations is pervasive, and it happens even to great leaders all the time. In fact, it's often one of the first things that leaps out to me when coaching clients.

Recently, one such client, a VP of Client Services named Ricardo, had encountered the age-old problem faced by so many in leadership: he was ready to move up the ladder, but he had no successor.

Or, as he put it, he had "90 percent" of a successor in one of his employees, Justine, but he couldn't get her to fully inhabit the leader role. Until she did, he couldn't leave the team in her hands.

"Justine has all the ingredients of a great VP," Ricardo told me. "She's smart, charismatic, her decisions are spot on, and the team already loves her."

The problem was that these strong traits didn't always come out when Justine was with clients. In his view, Justine tended to hang back in client meetings; she rarely spoke first when opinions were sought, and she often allowed the client to push through bad ideas rather than leading them to the solution that would actually serve them best.

"I need her to show up as a leader. I've been giving her this feedback consistently, and we've been coaching on it for months. She's not getting there. I'm starting to wonder if she ever will."

Secretly, I had a hunch why that might be the case. I had been coaching the entire Client Services team at this company for several months, and it wasn't the first time I had gotten the sense that Ricardo's expectation-setting had more in common with the pictogram instructions that come with an IKEA bookshelf. His grand vision was there, but when it came to the details, oftentimes, a lot of the little wooden pegs were missing.

I decided to reach out to Justine directly and set up a session with her. When the day arrived, I kicked off the discussion with a question:

"Justine, what does it mean to you to show up as a leader?"

Justine's reaction was exactly what I had anticipated. Rolling her eyes, she let out a frustrated sigh, one I could tell she'd been bottling up for a while.

"Honestly, Jackie? I'll be damned if I know!"

She filled me in on her perspective. When Ricardo had approached her about becoming a VP at the company, she'd been thrilled and eager to work on her missing "10 percent." She recalled the same phrasing Ricardo had said to me: "You have all the ingredients of a killer VP. I just need you to show up as a leader."

Great! But…what did that *mean*, exactly? Over the next few months, Justine had tried to figure it out, doing everything she could think of to "show up as a leader." She tried to exude more confidence. She spent more time preparing for meetings. She tried to speak with more authority, more gravity. She even paid attention to how she sat at the conference table.

None of it seemed to be what Ricardo was looking for. "I'm starting to think it's a mind game," Justine said. "He keeps dangling this carrot—I'm going to be a VP—and I throw myself after it, but nothing I do is ever good enough."

"Have you asked him for specifics?" I said. "I mean literally, as a bulleted list."

Justine frowned. "No," she said. "I've never done that…I feel like asking for specifics on how to be a leader would disqualify me entirely. If I have to be *told* what being a leader looks like, maybe I'm *not* one."

It was obvious to me, and obvious to Ricardo, for that matter, that Justine was a natural leader, and had all the makings of a great one. Yet here she was, totally deflated and doubting herself because she couldn't figure out what Ricardo wanted, and asking him outright felt like admitting defeat.

They were both stuck. And the organization was stuck along with them. The C-suite was missing a crucial chair at the table, and the Client Services team had a frustrated VP in Ricardo, itching to move up to his next position and feeling trapped in his current one.

NO CLARITY, NO RESULTS

What do Ted the car detailing manager and Ricardo have in common?

Despite being otherwise successful in their roles, they're both in the 50 percent of managers who don't set effective employee expectations. That number comes from a Towers Watson survey, and to me, it's staggering. *Fifty percent.* Half of all leaders out there are trying to drive results with a team that isn't clear on what they're supposed to be doing.

Yet hardly ever do I hear from leaders that the people they lead aren't "meeting expectations." The word "expectations" usually only comes up in a positive context: something like, "I have high expectations for my team." Typically, when expressing dissatisfaction, leaders I coach are more apt to say that they "aren't seeing" results, behaviors, or actions they want to see from their reports.

My answer is always the same: *Are you sure they know what you're looking for?*

As with everything we've discussed in this book so far, expectations are subject to perspective. It's entirely possible that leaders believe they're being crystal clear with expectations, while employees feel those expectations are murky at best.

Vague, unclear—or even more commonly, *unspoken*—expectations set off a cascade of emotional challenges for employees. Deep down, the majority of people in an organization want to succeed. They want to do their best. They want to pull their weight, they want to contribute, and they want to perform. Without clearly delineated expectations from their leader, employees have no way of knowing which direction they should aim their efforts; they're essentially flying blind.

The problem is less that employees have no idea what their job is, and more that they're unclear on what success in that job looks like, *according to their leader.*

That's the key part. Success, like everything else, is a matter of perspective. Without a leader who clearly states what they're looking for, employees are left to determine what success looks like via their own perspective and background of experience. They might draw their perspective of success from previous jobs, previous bosses. On a fundamental level, expectations diverge in ways neither party is aware of.

This can lead to incredible frustration and ultimately prevent leaders from connecting with the people they serve. When someone is working hard to succeed, but continually told they're missing the mark—or even when they're doing great, but that performance is rarely called out and celebrated—it can be demoralizing. They may feel like they're unable to do their best, that their efforts are invalidated. *What's the point in trying?* This is a quick road to employee disengagement; and with disengagement comes reduced performance, missed business goals, and ultimately, stagnation.

Expectations in Numbers

There are myriad reasons why expectations are so often unclear to employees, and as a leader, it's up to you to fix that. Here's a current look at the state of expectations in most workplaces:

- Ninety-seven percent of employees and executives believe lack of alignment within a team impacts the outcome of a task or project[23]—yet only 5.9 percent of companies communicate goals daily![24]

- Sixty percent of employees between the ages of eighteen and thirty-four report high levels of work-related stress, and "unrealistic expectations" is one of the top two causes cited.[25]

23 Meredith Wholley, "7 Workplace Collaboration Statistics and Advice," ClearCompany, September 3, 2017, https://blog.clearcompany.com/7-workplace-collaboration-statistics-that-will-have-you-knocking-down-cubicles.

24 Sara Pollock, "Final Destination: Organizational Transparency," ClearCompany, April 3, 2014, https://blog.clearcompany.com/final-destination-organizational-transparency.

25 Tom Starner, "Report: Millennials Reeling from 'Unrealistic' Workplace Demands," Human Resource Executive, May 29, 2019, https://hrexecutive.com/report-millennials-reeling-from-unrealistic-workplace-demands/.

- Fifty-one percent of job applicants reported "unrealistic expectations" as a top dealbreaker.[26]

- Only 22 percent of companies know what is driving employee disengagement![27]

"Unclear expectations" is the top source of employee frustration cited in study after study. A recent Gallup study validates the 50 percent finding from the Towers Watson survey, but from the other direction: worldwide, 50 percent of employees disagree that they know what's expected of them at work.[28] In the same study, Gallup measured engagement of those employees. They asked employees if they agree with the statement *My manager helps me set work priorities*. Of those who disagreed, only 4 percent ranked high in employee engagement (answering "agree" or "strongly agree" to statements like "I recommend this company as a good place to work").[29]

This means that *96 percent* of employees who are unclear on expectations are disengaged. They're likely not as invested in their work or committed to their role, and they are far more likely to be looking elsewhere for their next job.

---

26   "Seven Top Deal-Breakers When Applying for, Accepting a Job," Cision PR Newswire, December 10, 2019, https://www.prnewswire.com/news-releases/seven-top-deal-breakers-when-applying-for-accepting-a-job-300972497.html.

27   "The State of Talent Optimization," The Predictive Index, 2020, https://media.predictiveindex.com/legacy/wp-content/uploads/2020/01/TO_Benchmarking_Report.pdf.

28   Jim Harter, "Obsolete Annual Reviews: Gallup's Advice," Gallup, September 28, 2015, https://www.gallup.com/workplace/236567/obsolete-annual-reviews-gallup-advice.aspx.

29   Ibid.

A disengaged team is dead in the water when it comes to performance. Forget brilliance—any spark at all is going to fizzle right out.

KEY ACTIONS FOR GREAT EXPECTATIONS

As a leader, if you're misaligned with your team, it's most likely in one of these three ways:

1. You're focused on big-picture vision, and fail to communicate the details. Left to intuit those details for themselves, employees rely on their own perception of what success looks like. This might not match *your* perception of what success looks like. Employees deliver work or exhibit behaviors that they think are what you're looking for, but they continually miss your mark— because they don't know exactly what it is.

2. You *do* communicate the details, and you set very clear expectations. Unfortunately, those expectations are unrealistic. This presents a catch-22 for employees: either they admit they can't meet your expectations (which, to them, feels like saying "I'm not good enough"), or they silently struggle until they ultimately fail.

3. You don't communicate the details, nor much of anything when it comes to what you're thinking; you believe the work speaks for itself and that if you give a solid set of instructions, people should be able to execute. You struggle with connection in general as a leader (if this is you, believe me, you're not alone!).

Fixing or heading off any of the above scenarios involves the following three key actions. As the leader, these actions begin with you.

Action #1: Clarity Is Kind

Visionary thinking is essential in leadership; companies and employees count on their leaders to set ambitious goals, and thinking big is what drives an organization forward. The Big Hairy Audacious Goal, as Jim Collins coined it, is an incredible motivator for a team. Optimistic leaders believe in their team members, and reflect that belief outward so that the team believes in themselves, too. My client Lauren often says of her team, "I set the bar higher for my team than anyone else in the company, because I know they have it in them to reach it." Employees keenly sense the belief their leaders have in them, and much of that belief is communicated through the ambition of big-picture vision. *Yes, this goal is crazy. I know you can reach it. We're going to do it together.* Big-picture vision acts as an amplifier on a team's performance, spurring them to stretch, grow, and surprise themselves with their accomplishments.

The details, however, matter. Ricardo's missive to Justine was essentially a big-picture vision: *show up as a leader, and you'll be a great VP.* Justine was initially motivated by that vision and threw everything she had at it. But without the details, she fell short of the bar Ricardo had set. Meanwhile, Ricardo felt like his coaching was in vain; Justine "wasn't getting there."

Getting clear on expectations with your team begins with getting clear on the details. This looks like, first, making sure *you yourself* are clear on those details. After all, it begins with you.

Could Ricardo write out a bullet list of what "show up as a leader" meant?

I asked him to do so on the next video call we had.

He initially seemed confused. "I don't get it," he said. "Bullet list of what? Show up as a leader…everyone knows what that means. Be…a leader. Be…"

He paused, and I watched the wheels turning in his head, the fog of his false-consensus effect beginning to clear.

"It's hard to articulate," he said.

I nodded. "If it's hard for you to articulate, how easy do you think it is for Justine to understand?"

Over the rest of the call, we broke down what he meant by "show up as a leader," in real, actionable terms. By the end, I could tell that Ricardo was a little chagrined. He was starting to see that, in setting unclear expectations, he had nearly torpedoed his best shot at moving up to the C-suite, which was Justine taking on his role.

Action #2: Context Is Key

We've all been there: as a leader, you set a reach goal for your team that you feel is just aspirational enough to motivate them toward greater potential. Yet when you try to pump them up about the goal, they stare back at you blankly, totally nonplussed.

Goals that seem completely unrealistic are actually *demotivating*. But you can shift something that seems unrealistic to seeming totally within reach by simply giving your team the context behind the goal.

People want to understand not just *what* they're doing, but *why* they're doing it. Understanding the full picture of exactly how they're contributing to a goal reignites their motivation even when a goal seems too lofty. Context grounds something that feels impossible in real terms, bringing the person into the vision as a player, rather than a spectator.

Ricardo, for instance, had never told Justine *why* he was in a rush to get her to VP. He hadn't divulged that he was being promoted to the C-suite. Had he brought her into the vision and given her all the context, Justine might have understood that the goal wasn't hypothetical—*she was actually going to be doing Ricardo's job soon.* She would have had a much clearer idea of where she needed to level up by simply comparing her current performance to the standard Ricardo had established himself.

Always begin with yourself: are *you* clear on the why? If you aren't, how can you expect anyone on your team to be?

Action #3: Order of Priority

Recall what we discussed earlier: most employees, deep down, want to succeed. They want to perform. Effective prioritizing, however, rarely comes naturally to people, so it often looks like taking on a full plate of work and attacking it like the never-ending pasta bowl at Olive Garden. The best leaders understand that most employees need to be taught not just what their work *is*, but how to approach and knock out that work, and in what order.

Once you've gotten clear on the details and given the context for your expectations, ask your team for their plan to tackle it. Share your insights and direction so that they end up with a clear order and priority they should stick with in executing the vision. In these discussions, it's also important to align on what they currently have on their plates. Their existing priorities (often forgotten in the face of big-picture vision) are just as important to the equation as the new ones you're giving them. Take the time to discuss and mutually agree on a plan for how they're going to get things done. From there, they have a clear runway to take off.

BUSINESS BREAKTHROUGHS

As the saying goes, "People don't leave companies; people leave bosses." As mentioned earlier in this chapter, the top reported reason for employee stress and unhappiness is "unclear expectations"—and this unhappiness translates to high turnover, which costs businesses on average 33 percent of a departing employee's salary.[30] This drain of talent and money is hugely impacted by clear expectation-setting. Employees report that they are 23 percent more likely to stay at a company if their manager clearly explains their role and responsibilities.[31] And companies with engaged employees see 233 percent greater customer loyalty and a 26 percent greater annual increase in revenue.[32]

30   John Hall, "The Cost of Turnover Can Kill Your Business and Make Things Less Fun," *Forbes*, May 9, 2019, https://www.forbes.com/sites/johnhall/2019/05/09/the-cost-of-turnover-can-kill-your-business-and-make-things-less-fun/?sh=298836b47943.

31   Lori Li, "17 Surprising Statistics about Employee Retention," TINYpulse, September 8, 2020, https://www.tinypulse.com/blog/17-surprising-statistics-about-employee-retention.

32   Mike Hicks, "5 Ways to Build a Better Corporate Culture and Engage Employees," TalentCulture, July 18, 2017, https://talentculture.com/5-ways-build-better-corporate-culture-engage-employees/.

SHARED PERSPECTIVES

Ricardo and Justine's biggest roadblock wasn't in the details, the context, or the priorities.

It was in perspective.

This is where *alignment* comes in. Without articulating your perspective and hearing the other person's in return, there's little hope of getting on the same page.

When Ricardo next met with Justine, he apologized.

"I can see that I haven't been clear with you on my expectations, and I put you in a bad spot. Let me bring you in on the context first, and then I'll lay out exactly what I'm looking for."

Ricardo told me later that when he had divulged his upcoming promotion to Justine, her entire demeanor changed. She relaxed; her face lit up. "This makes so much sense!" she said.

Next up was clarifying for Justine what he still wasn't seeing in her leadership. He shared his perspective on her attitude and demeanor in client meetings. "When I meet with clients, I'm running the show," he told her. "I make sure they feel safe and well guided. We want them to feel like they don't have to do all the work, that they're in good hands."

Justine chewed her lip, a small smile in one corner of her mouth. "Is *that* right," she said.

When Ricardo asked what she meant, he was completely caught off guard by her response.

Justine had begun her career at the company in the call center. Her job had been to help clients solve problems, to listen to their feedback after the company's service was complete, and to measure customer satisfaction with NPS surveys. In the two years she'd spent in the call center before moving over to Client Services, Justine had come away with one prevailing understanding of how many of the company's clients felt.

Pushed around.

Even some of the most satisfied customers mentioned feeling talked over, rushed along, or pushed into decisions they weren't ready to make. They often felt like no one at the company really wanted to hear what they had to say, and that when they did speak up, they weren't heard.

So when Justine joined the Client Services team and became one of the front-line specialists meeting with clients, she took that feedback to heart in how she ran the meetings. She made it a point to always let the client lead the conversation. She listened fully to their perspective and verbally acknowledged that she heard them before sharing her own thoughts. She retained control of the decision-making—that was why her results spoke for themselves—but she did so while making the client feel like *they* had made the decision.

What Ricardo had seen as passive and permissive had been completely intentional. Her style was the opposite of Ricardo's, but as he told me on our next call, "I think it's probably *better*. If I'm honest, her client retention is higher than mine. I was looking for someone to be the next me—but the person the company really needs in that role is Justine!"

That meeting was a turning point for both Ricardo and Justine. By sharing their perspectives on the situation and getting on the same page, they were able to closely align to the mission: both of them getting well-deserved promotions, and the Client Services team entering a new phase of leadership that would level them up even more.

EXPECTING BRILLIANCE

As a leader, you hold the keys to your team's performance.

Aligned expectations feel like flow. Everyone is clear, motivated, and moving in the same direction. Productivity soars; people feel like they're doing their best, making the grade. You'll see people spark in ways you hadn't anticipated. Remember—*they want to perform*. They just need you to clearly lay out what performance means to you, help them envision the *why* behind the goals, and determine a structure of priorities that sets them up for success.

At the heart of aligning on expectations is Platinum Leadership. Individually, with each team member, get on the same page when it comes to both of your perspectives on the goals, details, and priorities of the company, the team, and their own unique role. What they share might surprise you—and help you reach the next level of your own leadership journey.

Recently, after hearing Rob tell his car-detailing story to another group of friends, I asked him if he'd ever figured out what his old manager could have been looking for. Had the magical secret to Q-tip nirvana finally been exposed to him since the first and last time he was fired?

He laughed.

"To this day, I have no idea what he could have meant," he said. "In thirty years, I've never seen a car that was as shiny or dust-free as the last car I detailed before I was canned. Then again, Ted spent all day breathing in clouds of toxic fumes, so who knows…maybe we were both hallucinating."

YOU GET SOLID: SELF-EVALUATION

1. What does success look like in your role?

2. How would your own leader answer that question?

3. What are the five most important actions you can take to achieve success?

4. Are you clear on your company and team's mission? Its vision? Its purpose?

5. What's the why behind that vision?

6. What are the top priorities in achieving that vision?

7. What might need to be deprioritized in order to keep everyone focused and aligned?

THEY GET SOLID: NEXT STEPS

1. Ask team members to write down the top three priorities of the company, the team, and their own role.

2. Review the answers with each team member individually, getting on the same page with details, context, and priority-resetting as needed.

4

CONNECT

According to Gallup, companies lose $360 billion in productivity every year as a result of poor relationships between employees and their leaders.[33]

"I feel like I'm right back where I started. Except this time, I have no idea what to do."

Nathan, the CMO of a rapidly expanding advertising agency, had already been working with me for over a year by the time March of 2020 rolled around. In that year, he'd worked hard and made massive improvements in his relationships with his team members. But the pandemic, with the sudden shift to physical isolation and remote work, had thrown him for a loop.

The year of coaching we'd done together had focused on relationships and connection. Nathan was a natural achiever, and his results as CMO spoke for themselves. But the employees within the Marketing division consistently returned low ratings on connection in company surveys. He

---

33 Sagrika Mehta, "Coaching for Managers: The Roadway to Drive 10x Results and Build a High-Performing Culture," Peoplebox, https://www.peoplebox.ai/blog/coaching-for-managers/.

was great at leading his team to execute vision and clear consistently higher bars, but when it came to the individual relationships he had with team members, in many ways, it wasn't his strongest skill.

A natural introvert, and a quiet, more reserved presence, Nathan envied the other leaders in his company who always seemed to have such easy rapport with their employees.

"It's like they're able to create conversations out of thin air," he told me in one of our first sessions. "There's always some point of connection they just seem to magically *know* about. People's favorite sports teams, their kids, the TV shows they're watching at that moment. How do they have the time to learn all these personal things about their team members? And how do they remember all of it?"

I've heard the same thing from many, many clients I've worked with. To those who aren't natural connectors, watching someone who *is* a natural connector feels like watching a magician performing a card trick. You start with a fair bit of skepticism: *Okay, sure, I know what they're doing here, they're shuffling twice and they're holding their thumb on that one part of the deck. Next they're going to—*

With no warning, the trick turns on its head. The sought-after card appears out of thin air, not from the deck, but from inside an audience member's pocket. You're left baffled.

How on earth did they DO that?

Nathan had tried to replicate what he saw other leaders doing, and his results were…shall we say, somewhat less robust than the pipeline full of smoking-hot leads his marketing team's campaigns delivered for the company.

Even I had to cringe when he told me his most mortifying moment yet—walking up behind an employee as she poured herself some coffee, blurting out loudly, "What fun things do you have planned this weekend?" only to startle her into spilling the coffee all over herself.

When we began our coaching sessions, Nathan had convinced himself that to be a connector, he had to change his personality. He was hyperfocused on being more outgoing, more gregarious, funnier, friendlier.

"So, remember back in grade school, what our parents always told us was the best way to make friends?" I said to him. *"Be yourself."*

Nathan didn't need to become someone he wasn't. He was kind, well-liked, and well-respected. Team members often said they appreciated the contrast of his calmer energy with some of the more fiery presences on the executive team. He set clear expectations, responded quickly when support was needed, and set a standard of excellence his team was proud to be a part of. He had a great foundation built for the team as a whole—he just needed to work on individual relationships.

By March of 2020, Nathan and I had spent a year creating and sowing a practice of repeatable habits that would form the authentic connections he sought. We'd seen many of those seeds begin to sprout already. One particularly fruitful practice had been simple note-taking. Nathan had begun carrying a small notebook with him. At the beginning of each meeting or gathering, he forced himself to stay super present and truly absorb all of the personal chitchat and sharing that happened naturally between employees before the meeting started. He jotted it down in his notebook. Then, anytime he had interactions with employees later on, he'd review those personal details he'd jotted down so that he could build connection at the top of the conversation (good old Power Lead at work!). *How was*

*your daughter's dance recital? I heard you're taking a trip to France—
what have you got planned? Hey, I didn't know you went to Berkeley for
grad school; so did I!*

Within a few months of trying this out, he saw his employees subtly shift
their attitude toward him. It had never been negative, but now it was
blossoming from simple, professional work discussions into a vibe of
connection. He received more invitations to happy hours, more casual
walks over lunch. Over the course of the year, his relationships built real
traction. He even noticed that new hires were quicker to warm to him.

In his own way, as his own person, Nathan had begun to get a feel for
fostering connection.

And then, all of a sudden, the rug got pulled out from under his feet.

When the pandemic hit hard in March of 2020, Nathan's entire company—
like nearly every company in his industry—went fully remote as people
locked down in their houses and prepared to work from home for the
indefinite future.

Within just a couple of weeks, Nathan saw all the connection sprouts he'd
nurtured for the past year wither and die.

"I've realized that I relied so much on being in the same room with people
to form connections," he told me on our first coaching session after the
lockdown had begun, obviously stressed. "With the computer screen
between us now, I don't even know where to start. It's harder to read
their energy. I'm not able to make casual observations—I only ever see
them on scheduled Zoom meetings. They feel a million miles away, even
though we all live in the same city."

He sighed and raked a hand through his hair. He had the dark circles under his eyes I'd seen on so many clients in those first weeks of the pandemic.

"If I thought finding time for relationships was hard before, it feels almost impossible now," he said. "How am I going to keep everyone feeling connected when we're all just faces on a laptop screen?"

It was the same question a dozen different clients had asked me that week. The answer was simple, but not easy.

Understanding connection begins with understanding *authenticity*. And authenticity begins with you, the leader. It's entirely within your control.

If you can show up authentically, connection will flow from that authenticity no matter where you and your team are physically located.

BUSINESS BREAKTHROUGHS

Authentic connection in teams makes them stronger—and leads to greater business outcomes across the board. An authentic workplace is a top desire of engaged employees, with 75 percent saying they want their coworkers to share more about their true selves.[34] Teams that report a strong sense of connection correlate to vastly higher employee engagement ratings; organizations

---

34 Vanessa Buote, "Most Employees Feel Authentic at Work, but It Can Take a While," *Harvard Business Review*, May 11, 2016, https://hbr.org/2016/05/most-employees-feel-authentic-at-work-but-it-can-take-a-while.

that score highest on employee engagement are an average of 21 percent more profitable.[35]

CULTURE THEATER GETS BAD REVIEWS

There's nothing like a good icebreaker to open up a group and get communication flowing.

However, there's a *right* way to use an icebreaker, and there's definitely a wrong way—and in my experience, the wrong way tends to happen far too often in many companies and teams.

A great icebreaker comes from the intention to build or deepen authentic connection. But when an icebreaker feels forced and inauthentic, it's one of the most ineffective devices used in workplace communication. When connection feels like *forced* connection, it rarely comes off as anything but awkward.

On a larger scale, I see this effect all the time in corporations with disengaged and demotivated cultures. These companies try to improve employee engagement and connection by bringing in what I call "culture theater": happy hours, foosball tables, Taco Tuesday, and the like. Perks like this are nice when you *already have* a connection culture—but when used as a band-aid to wallpaper over dissatisfaction, they're met with a shrug. On their own, they don't create real connection. Culture theater is a performance, not a relationship.

---

35 "8 Employee Engagement Statistics You Need to Know in 2021," Smarp, Jan 4, 2021, https://blog.smarp.com/employee-engagement-8-statistics-you-need-to-know.

If you sought out this book, you're almost certainly the type of leader who understands how ineffective culture theater is, and you probably have an instinctive understanding of what truly *does* create a lasting, deeply motivating, and engaging culture: *authentic connection.*

A recent Gallup study found that the vast majority of an individual's engagement at work is driven by their manager.[36] Daniel Goleman, the author of *Emotional Intelligence,* coined a phrase that describes the relationship between employee and leader: a "vertical couple." When the bond between the vertical couple is strong, the employee's productivity rises. They're more engaged; they're less likely to look for another role elsewhere.

Key Concept: Emotional Contagion

Where the Platinum Leadership framework focuses is on the contagion created by the mood, outlook, and behavior of you, the leader. We know that the team will pick up on each other's negativity, anxiety, and stress, and with no one is this more true than with the team's leader.

The best way to make the concept of emotional contagion click for someone is to tell them, "Imagine yawning."

There—you just yawned, didn't you?

---

36 Randall Beck and Jim Harter, "Managers Account for 70% of Variance in Employee Engagement," *Gallup Business Journal*, April 21, 2015, https://news.gallup.com/businessjournal/182792/managers-account-variance-employee-engagement.aspx.

Much to the delight of kids throughout the ages, the act of yawning is probably the most universally recognized as wickedly contagious for seemingly no good reason. You look at someone yawning, you yawn. You think of someone yawning, you yawn. You can't help it. And if you try not to yawn, the impulse just gets worse.

It turns out that emotions function in almost exactly the same way and are just as contagious. Emotional contagion is the spontaneous transfer of emotions from one person to another or through a group. It was first written about back in 1911 by American psychologist James Baldwin, who called the phenomenon "contagion of feeling."[37] Throughout the past century, it was studied in countless ways, and in 1993, psychologists Elaine Hatfield, John Cacioppo, and Richard Rapson pinned down the concept as "the tendency to automatically mimic and synchronize expressions, vocalizations, postures, and movements with those of another person's and consequently, to converge emotionally."[38]

Researchers have documented how, as we pass through the day, our brains continually process the feelings of those around us. We notice the inflection of their voice, the arch of their eyebrows, the slope of their shoulders. Our amygdala can read and identify

---

37 James Baldwin, *The Individual and Society or Psychology and Sociology* (Boston: Richard G. Badger, 1911), 44.

38 Elaine Hatfield, John T. Cacioppo, and Richard L. Rapson, "Emotional Contagion," *Current Directions in Psychological Science* 2 no. 3 (June 1993): 96–99, https://www.jstor.org/stable/20182211.

emotions in another person's face in 33 milliseconds[39] and almost instantaneously prime us to adopt that emotion as well. This all happens subconsciously, but consciously we're doing the same thing: reading people and feeling the same thing they're feeling. If you put three strangers in a room, the most emotionally expressive individual will transmit their mood to the others within two minutes.

So, to put it simply, when someone in a bad mood enters your sphere, you suddenly find yourself in a bad mood, too. The effect is amplified in groups, and it doesn't even require physical presence to occur. In January of 2012, Facebook conducted an experiment (the ethicality of which has been widely debated) that manipulated the content of 689,003 users' news feeds.[40] Some people were bombarded with positive news stories, happy life updates, and words that had been determined to be more positive. Other people were shown an onslaught of content that had been categorized as more negative and pessimistic. After a week of this content delivery, the groups of users were prompted to make their own posts. Predictably, those users in the Positive group spontaneously posted more positive status messages; those in the Negative group posted gloom.

---

39 Rachel Feltman, "Your Brain Helps You Judge a Face Before You Even See It," *The Washington Post*, August 5, 2014, https://www.washingtonpost.com/news/speaking-of-science/wp/2014/08/05/your-brain-helps-you-judge-a-face-before-you-even-see-it/.

40 Robinson Meyer, "Everything We Know about Facebook's Secret Mood-Manipulation Experiment," *The Atlantic*, September 8, 2014, https://www.theatlantic.com/technology/archive/2014/06/everything-we-know-about-facebooks-secret-mood-manipulation-experiment/373648/.

If people in digital groups can so easily be infected by emotions, what does that suggest for groups of people who work together every day in the same office space?

Recall Lauren's anxious breakdown about the downward slide of her team's emotional climate. I hate how I'm showing up. This is not how I work. She was so steeped in an emotional space of mistrust, confusion, fear, and disappointment that her team couldn't help but catch those emotions like a bad cold.

And as I coached Lauren to understand, the way she got into that situation was also the way she would get out of it. They followed her there, and they would follow her somewhere new.

The impact a positive-minded leader can have has been borne out by research. When leaders are optimistic and inspired, their employees are much more likely to be in a good mood too. What's more, employees will exhibit more social helping behaviors to their coworkers and coordinate work better.

With every moment of your interactions with the people you lead, you have the opportunity to create a ripple effect with your outlook and emotional state. You have the power to use emotional contagion to the benefit of everyone around you. A leader's prevailing demeanor permeates an entire company. Good, high-level leaders full of optimism inspire the same from their mid-level reports, and those people pass it along to the people below them. Before long, the sense of possibility cascades through an organization, activating a high-performing, highly fulfilled, motivated, and energetic culture.

According to the *Harvard Business Review*, even in our new remote-inclusive work landscape, one-on-ones between employees and leaders remain vital to employee success. In the companies they analyzed, the average manager spent thirty minutes every three weeks with each of their employees. Perhaps unsurprisingly, employees who got little to no one-on-one time with their manager were more likely to be disengaged. On the flip side, those who get twice the number of one-on-ones with their manager relative to their peers are 67 percent less likely to be disengaged.[41] HBR also tested the hypothesis that there would be a point at which engagement goes down if a manager spends *too much* time with employees—surprise, surprise, that tipping point doesn't exist!

In contrast, employees who don't have one-on-ones with their managers are four times as likely to be disengaged as individual contributors as a whole, and are two times as likely to view leadership more unfavorably compared to those who meet with their managers regularly.[42]

---

41 Ryan Fuller and Nina Shikaloff, "What Great Managers Do Daily," *Harvard Business Review*, December 14, 2016, https://hbr.org/2016/12/what-great-managers-do-daily.

42 Ibid.

The connection of the *team* is a crucial piece of the puzzle, too. People who report having friends at work consistently rank higher in both happiness and performance. This shouldn't come as a surprise; we spend at least forty hours a week at work, so creating strong relationships and even friendships at work keeps those forty hours engaging and motivating.

Authentic Connection in Numbers

- Mentorships matter: employees with mentors are five times more likely to be promoted than people without mentors.[43]

- Seventy-six percent of workers agree that empathy in the workplace drives productivity.[44]

- Remote work is here to stay, and that changes your role as the leader. Sixty percent of workers report feeling alone and isolated while working remotely.[45]

- Even before the pandemic, 76 percent of executives surveyed worldwide reported having difficulty

---

43   James C. Price, "The Case for Mentorship," Refresh Leadership, August 31, 2020, http://www.refreshleadership.com/index.php/2020/08/case-mentorship/.

44   "2020 State of Workplace Empathy," Businessolver, 2020, https://www.businessolver.com/workplace-empathy-executive-summary.

45   Brent Orrell and Matthew Leger, "Lonely and Stressed: How Working from Home Is Affecting Americans' Mental Health," *USA Today*, March 3, 2021, https://www.usatoday.com/story/opinion/2021/03/03/working-home-pandemic-has-left-americans-lonely-and-stressed-column/6883765002/.

feeling connected to their teammates on distributed teams.[46]

- The probability of dying early is 20 percent higher for obese people, 30 percent higher for excessive drinkers, 50 percent higher for smokers, but a whopping 70 percent higher for people with poor social relationships.[47]

- Fifty-two percent of employees exiting their roles say that their manager could have done something to prevent them from leaving their job. Nevertheless, only 51 percent of employees who left their job had a conversation about their engagement, development, or future during the three months leading up to their departure.[48]

- Naturally great managers and leaders build relationships that create trust, open dialogue, and full transparency.[49]

46   Mark Mortensen, "Four Ways Today's Teams Are Making Us Lonely," INSEAD, April 19, 2021, https://knowledge.insead.edu/leadership-organisations/four-ways-todays-teams-are-making-us-lonely-16466.

47   Emma Seppälä and Kim Cameron, "Proof That Positive Work Cultures Are More Productive," *Harvard Business Review*, December 1, 2015, https://hbr.org/2015/12/proof-that-positive-work-cultures-are-more-productive.

48   Ben Wigert and Ellyn Maese, "How Your Manager Experience Shapes Your Employee Experience," Gallup, July 9, 2019, https://www.gallup.com/workplace/259469/manager-experience-shapes-employee-experience.aspx.

49   Bailey Nelson, "How to Help Every Manager Be More Like a Natural Leader," Gallup, June 17, 2019, https://www.gallup.com/workplace/258194/help-every-manager-natural-leader.aspx.

CONNECTION IS CARE

Great relationships make us happier and better at our work. On a deeper level, though, they help us thrive as humans.

Research shows that the greatest predictor of our happiness and long-term success as humans is the relationships we build. This is supported by a Harvard study[50] that focuses on happiness and what contributes to it. Incredibly, this study has been going on for more than eighty years, and in that time, it has found that social bonds not only predict overall happiness, health, and longevity, but also play a role in our career achievements, occupational success, and income.

Good relationships—deep, authentic bonds—don't just protect the body; they also protect the brain and spirit. This was evident to researchers again and again over the years as they interviewed participants, took blood tests, and tracked everything from marriage and divorce to jobs, careers, and illness. The consistent finding was that your background, origin, or opportunities—the hand of cards you were dealt in life—had far less of an impact on your overall happiness than the quality of your relationships. Relationship quality has even been positively correlated with how long you live, how successful you feel, and how much money you make over the course of your career.

When I think about the power of workplace connections, I think about *The Office*. Yes, it's fiction, but even so, there's a lot to be learned amid the rapid-fire hilarity. The boss, Michael Scott, is a total buffoon, and swings wildly between merely annoying and totally inappropriate.

---

50   Matthew Solan, "The Secret to Happiness? Here's Some Advice from the Longest-Running Study on Happiness," Harvard Health Publishing, October 5, 2017, https://www.health.harvard.edu/blog/the-secret-to-happiness-heres-some-advice-from-the-longest-running-study-on-happiness-2017100512543.

(There's unexpected nudity, there's deeply offensive language—there's a moment where he runs an employee down with his car.) By all evidence, his employees should *loathe* him.

And yet—every time Michael experiences a disappointment, or needs support, his employees begrudgingly pat him on the back and pick him up again. Why? Because Michael, despite all his clownish insanity, *takes the time* to know each of them and form personal connections. (Except with Toby. Never Toby.) They respond with connection in return.

Take the episode where Pam is showing her art in a local gallery show. Despite inviting all of her coworkers, no one shows up. She stands alone for hours, increasingly upset and embarrassed. Just as she's packing up, Michael appears, having "raced across town" to attend. He moves her to tears by being blown away by her work, asking to buy one piece, and telling her how proud he is of her. The time he takes to authentically build his connection with her is priceless. It ultimately leads to her giving him a break the next time he steps way out of bounds (which happens all of thirty seconds later, obviously, because it's a comedy and the episode runtime is only twenty-two minutes).

Powerful connections help us more happily navigate our jobs and workplaces. Studies have found that employees who have positive connections with their colleagues return to resting cardiovascular levels faster when facing moments of stress, a phenomenon called *work recovery*. Positive connections at work increase oxytocin, a hormone and neurotransmitter often associated with the powerful bond between mothers and newborns. Oxytocin in the brain acts to regulate emotional responses and promote positive social behaviors like trust, empathy, bonding, and positive communication.

Oxytocin also works to lower cortisol levels, allowing people to manage work-related stress, both in the moment and in the future. Even better, when a person enjoys strong bonds at work, they're less likely to feel stress in the first place. They become more optimistic; they see struggles at work as more of an opportunity to grow than as a crushing weight dragging them down.

Your job as a leader is to craft authentic connections with the people you lead. When a team member has a positive relationship with their leader, their motivation and performance increase. Strongly bonded, authentic relationships with your team members will allow you to discover and focus on their strengths, spot and celebrate wins, provide meaningful feedback, and listen to understand.

Leadership *is* connection.

Approaching connection the right way is crucial. Done right, it's one of the most powerful tools in your leadership toolkit. Done wrong, though, it only serves to reinforce the walls people build around themselves— walls that keep them feeling protected, but also make communication and collaboration that much more challenging.

The key differentiator between approaching connection the *right way* and *wrong way* is authenticity.

Authenticity can't be manufactured. It can't be fabricated. By definition, it's organic; it has to come from you naturally, not as the result of a step-by-step formula.

Authenticity arises from the deep-down desire to truly know and be known by others.

BE SEEN, BE KNOWN, BELONG

Quick question before we continue:

What's your *Harry Potter* house? Gryffindor, Ravenclaw, Hufflepuff, Slytherin?

I'd be willing to bet that most of you reading this book know exactly what your house is, because over the past couple of decades, you've likely taken—or at least seen, or been sent by a friend—any one of the countless online quizzes that place you in your Hogwarts house based on your personality traits. (And in case it isn't abundantly clear so far in how much I've talked about loving school and studying, I'm a Ravenclaw.)

Okay, maybe you've never taken that particular quiz. So, next question: which character from *Friends* are you?

Or, which Marvel Avenger—or villain—are you most like?

Or, what breed of dog are you?

I'd be hard pressed to count all the silly, fun online quizzes I've taken over the years—everything from which breakfast food best represents my personality (chocolate croissant) to which decade I was meant to live in (clearly the 80s, for everyone who knows me well).

Why do we love online quizzes?

As fun as they are, and as much as we all know they don't hold much meaning—they still make us feel seen. They make us feel *known*.

I need to take a little responsibility here. Because if you've been inundated over the course of your internet lifetime with dozens of random quizzes your friends tag you on, or that pop up in your social feeds... well, I'm one of the people you have to thank for that. (You're welcome. Or, sorry.)

Back in my mid-twenties, when I'd just finished grad school, a couple of fellow grads from Harvard Business School approached me to join their new startup, Emode. Emode was built on the concept that insights into human psychology and behavior could be freely collected online through quizzes—and the feedback would create a system for understanding human motivation. These insights could be applied to product development and marketing, helping new products go viral.

At the time, this idea was groundbreaking, and as a student of psychology, I eagerly jumped at the opportunity to help shape a system for collecting data on human behavior and motivations. I became Emode's Head of Content Development. I had no idea what I was doing yet, but neither did any of us; we were just a bunch of kids in a basement in Cambridge.

Our team created and launched little quizzes and personality tests that were similar to, at the time, the kind of thing you'd see in *Cosmopolitan* magazine—but applying more research and psychology to drive a real insightful result, rather than just offer entertainment. The quizzes were fun, often pop-culture-oriented, and highly shareable (but this was *long* before social media, so pasting the link into email was the most popular way they would be shared).

The very first quiz I created was "What Breed of Dog Are You?" I based the quiz questions and scoring on personality research, dog research, and anything else I thought would tease out the kind of results we were looking for: people giving input on their deepest likes, dislikes, behavior, and motivations.

When we put that first quiz on the internet, we had no expectation whatsoever of how much attention it would get.

To our utter shock, people went *nuts*.

It spread like wildfire. Within a few weeks, the link to our quiz was—*no exaggeration*—the most widely clicked link *in the entire world.*

"What Breed of Dog Are You?" ultimately settled to a daily unique visit rate of one million visitors per *day.* For 1999, this was like winning ten Super Bowls. It was completely unprecedented. The *New York Times* wrote an article about the popularity of the quiz. We got tons of media attention. And before long, lo and behold—a Bay Area venture capital firm came calling. Emode scored first-round funding, became Tickle. com, and a handful of us moved out to San Francisco.

I went on to write nearly one hundred quizzes for Tickle.com. Each one dug in deeper and deeper to how people truly thought about themselves and how they understood and perceived their inner world. It was the ultimate continuation of what I had learned in Dr. Duckworth's class: understanding somebody else's understanding, so that you know how they want to be treated. The quizzes were essentially a Platinum Rule vehicle.

It was work that I loved. No matter how fun or frothy the subject of a quiz was, it still represented a moment for someone to sit down, self-reflect, and understand themselves better—even if all they thought they were doing was having fun. I was deeply fulfilled by bringing that opportunity to people. So deeply fulfilled, in fact, that I knew I wanted it to be the basis of my career: helping people find self-awareness.

All the insights we learned through the quizzes we delivered coalesced into one prevailing theme: people *love* learning about themselves. What's more, they love validating things they suspect about themselves. They love the feeling of being seen, known, and understood.

Sharing what seems like a silly quiz result actually feels like sharing a piece of themselves. It's a way of saying to the world: *I want to know me, and I want you to know me. I want you to understand my understanding. Here are new words, symbols, and avatars we can share to understand each other better.*

At its root, this sharing represents connection. People want to be known—because being known opens up the opportunity to *belong*.

ACTIVE AUTHENTICITY

Building authentic connection isn't always easy when we're leading large teams. Even the leaders I coach who are great natural connectors often experience uncertainty when replicating the natural, easy relationships they have with individuals across an entire organization. And authentic connections become an even *bigger* challenge when you're not able to physically be in the same room as the people you're trying to connect with.

Like, say, when your entire seventy-five-person team goes from a bustling, energetic office environment one day to virtual house arrest the next.

So, where does authenticity begin?

Action #1: Magic in the Moments, Not the Meetings

When the pandemic hit, Nathan was stymied by the disappearance of his reliable people-watching time before meetings. It's something I heard from dozens of other clients, who realized that the interstitial space *between* meetings is where so much personal connection magic in their workplace had happened. There are ways to recreate that magic, though, even when you're not in person. One client began each meeting with a five-minute breakout session where everyone had to answer a question, solve a quick puzzle, tell a joke, share a win from the day—anything that got them connecting on a personal level before the group dived into the meeting agenda.

As I write this, many of us are back at work in person, and that personal connection piece becomes a little simpler, but still just as intentional. Get to meetings early so you can soak up the chitchat. Offer your next one-on-one to take a quick stretch-your-legs walk in lieu of sitting down in the conference room. Find ways to build space for the little magic moments that happen in between the work getting done.

Action #2: Be Present

Connection is best thought of as a verb, not a noun—it's an action. It can't happen without you giving your full attention to each present moment. This means that in each meeting, you have an opportunity to show your team members that they have your 100 percent full attention. Put down the phone—in fact, don't even bring it in the room! Create and maintain eye contact. Find a way to capture notes that doesn't have you glued to your computer screen. Connect with the person in the present, rather than looking to the future after the meeting.

Action #3: Ask Questions

The bottom line of communication, which we've talked about previously: be curious! Connection is built through curiosity. Ask people questions about themselves; seek to discover what's going on inside, how they're perceiving things, what they most deeply want and need. You don't need to read minds—just ask. Most important, when they do respond, be present in the response. Connect through making them feel seen and heard.

Influencing Up

As leaders, we know it's our job to develop genuine connections with those on our team. Those connections are crucial to improving performance. But building relationships with those above us on the corporate ladder or board is equally important to growing your career. After all, true leadership means influencing in every direction, including sideways and upward—and it's also how we affect true cultural change in an organization.

A client of mine, Caitlin, was challenged by her supervisor to develop more influence and connections with people above her in all parts of the organization during the COVID pandemic. She was told that that was how the executives decided who got promoted. "It's the people they know personally or who they've heard about. It's the people whose names keep coming up in meetings. There's a buzz about them. People know their name, and know what they've accomplished off the top of their head. It creates the sense that you're coming in hot and capable of handling more."

Caitlin was initially thrown. How am I going to network with people who have never met me while we're all working from home? Building authentic connections in person is hard, but pulling it off over Teams sounded even more daunting. How could she come across as sincere under such contrived circumstances?

She succeeded by being honest. We picked eight executives for her to contact, and she reached out to one of them every week over the course of two months. She began by introducing herself over email: "Because we're not in person and I won't have an opportunity to meet you organically thanks to COVID, I would love to have a call to introduce myself, learn more about your area of the business and what you're working on, and just connect," she wrote. "I'm really trying to build connections in a world where it's just not easy!"

Even though the process might not have felt authentic at first, Caitlin was authentic within the parameters at her disposal—and she made herself vulnerable in sharing the struggles they could all relate to. As she met with each one of these executives one by one over the next eight weeks, she came away feeling they knew her better and would have a much easier time connecting in the future when the world did open up. The executives, in turn, were impressed with her proactive approach; they admired her intent to grow her network and relationships even in such a tough time. It made her stand out and expand her net of internal champions—and she was able to do it while staying true to herself. What's more, she created a step-by-step process for the meetings so they stopped feeling so nerve-wracking for her. Because of this, she was able to return to work with the road paved for a stronger connection to the higher-ups in her company.

THE CONNECTION NEW NORMAL

Remember the "culture theater" from earlier in this chapter—the "hey, this is a *super* cool company, we swear!" hail marys thrown by out-of-touch leaders unwilling to put the extra effort in to engage with people individually to discover how they actually *want* to be treated? The foosball tables, cold brew on tap, catered lunches, and "team-building events" that, for many companies, are the primary examples of their culture—and beneath that facade, employees are dissatisfied, disengaged, downright unhappy?

None of that will make the leap to our new, rapidly evolving work landscape.

Even now, as I write this eighteen months into the pandemic, dozens of studies have been conducted on how it's fundamentally altered the way we work. The conclusions are clear: we've entered a whole new world of workplace culture, and it's not likely that things will ever "reset."

Our new work landscape includes flex time, hybrid remote/office work, and a totally shifted mindset when it comes to creating a connected, engaged culture. It also creates unique opportunities for even *deeper* connections, fueled by what seems like a paradoxical *increase* in authenticity.

If you're like my client Nathan, you might still be stumped on how authenticity could possibly be improved through the cold artificial light of your computer screen.

The Microsoft Work Trend Index recently conducted a massive study on the changing shape of our work landscape. Satya Nadella, CEO at Microsoft, reported: "Over the past year, no area has undergone more rapid transformation than the way we work. Employee expectations are changing, and we will need to define productivity much more broadly—inclusive of collaboration, learning, and wellbeing to drive career advancement for every worker, including frontline and knowledge workers, as well as for new graduates and those who are in the workforce today. All this needs to be done with flexibility in when, where, and how people work."[51] And while most business leaders actually found themselves thriving during remote work, those just starting out in their careers found themselves struggling with fewer in-person networking opportunities.

And yet the opportunity for greater connection is there—as long as you reset your expectations and approach it with optimism and an open mind. "Before the pandemic, we encouraged people to 'bring their whole self to work,' but it was tough to truly empower them to do that. The shared vulnerability of this time has given us a huge opportunity to bring real

---

51   Microsoft, "The Next Disruption Is Hybrid Work—Are We Ready?" *World Trend Index: 2021 Annual Report*, March 22, 2021, https://www.microsoft.com/en-us/worklab/work-trend-index/hybrid-work?hss_channel=tw-224412878.

authenticity to company culture and transform work for the better," said Jared Spataro, Corporate VP at Microsoft 365.[52] Compared to one year ago, 39 percent of people say they're more likely to be their full, authentic selves at work and 31 percent are less likely to feel embarrassed or ashamed when their home life shows up at work. And people who interacted with their coworkers more closely than before not only experienced stronger work relationships, but also reported higher productivity and better overall well-being.[53]

The Microsoft Work Trend Index reported the following on the year 2020:

> As people navigated unprecedented stress on the frontlines, balanced childcare and homeschool, worked from living rooms, quieted barking dogs, and pushed away curious cats, something changed: work became more human.

> One in five have met their colleagues' pets or families virtually, and as we clung to each other to get through the year, one in six (17 percent) have cried with a colleague this year.[54]

When Nathan initially felt dejected, discouraged, and lost in the face of his changed work environment, we worked together to focus on what mattered most in connecting with his team: authenticity. He'd tried a few remote team-building activities he'd heard about from other leaders, like digital happy hours, but they hadn't had the same effect as the natural connection his team had in person.

---

52 Ibid.

53 Ibid.

54 Ibid.

"Before, you'd observe your people at the office, removed from their homes," I told him. "What opportunity might there be in the fact that now you're seeing them in their own environments? What nuggets can you pull out of what you're seeing behind them, in the rooms beyond the Teams window?"

Nathan struggled at first. He was so focused on the in-person connections he wasn't making that he couldn't make space for a connection made digitally.

I reminded him that it began with him, and it began with authenticity. "Nathan, what's something in your own home environment that really makes you *you?*"

I saw a light bulb go off in his eyes. "Well, there was a moment recently during a meeting when I felt a little spark of the connection we used to have in the office," he said.

He told me the story: he'd been leading the team through their quarterly goal-setting. It was an intense discussion, full of brainstorming, breakdowns of details, and healthy disagreement and collaboration. When they were in the office, he'd made these quarterly planning sessions formal and highly focused so that they were super productive. He wanted everyone to stay on track to leave the room with clear expectations for the quarter ahead, and no confusion about their priorities.

When he ran the session over Zoom, the tone was still serious and productive, but the team struggled with focus. And it was all the fault of his cat, Henry.

Nathan's close friends often made the joke that Henry was the wingman Nathan never knew he needed. Unlike shy, reserved Nathan,

Henry had to be the center of attention. This usually looked like jumping into laps and refusing to budge; aggressive rubbing up against people's ankles; and a vocal, yowling insistence on being constantly petted.

That day during quarterly planning, every third sentence out of Nathan's mouth was interrupted by Henry rocketing himself up onto Nathan's desk and placing himself directly in front of the webcam. The first time his furry, gray-striped form and inquisitive green eyes had filled the frame, the team had erupted into surprised laughter—their usually ultraprofessional, emotionally reserved leader having a cat with such an opposite personality was the funniest thing that had happened in weeks (to be fair, the bar was especially low in those first dark pandemic months). Nathan's flustered apology and quick relocation of Henry via an unceremonious toss to the floor made it even funnier. And each time Henry jumped up and took over the meeting, Nathan's increasing desperation just made the team laugh more.

Pretty soon, the agenda had evaporated, other team members started holding up their own animals to the screen, and the coos and *omg, so cute!*s completely derailed the meeting. Nathan gave in to the madness and allowed a brief ten-minute intermission wherein each team member introduced their pets to an adoring audience.

"At first, I was so tense and annoyed—I like things to stay professional and on track," Nathan said. "But then I realized that I was seeing the team smile and laugh together, truly connect, for the first time in weeks. It was the same connection we had from the office, but in an entirely different form."

"Do you think it would have had the same effect if it hadn't been spontaneous?" I asked. "For instance, if you'd planned a pet show-and-tell as a connection activity?"

He shook his head. "I don't think so. I think they would have had fun, but it was the connection with *me* that really took it next level. When Henry jumped up on the screen, it was a part of me they'd never seen before. I was being real in a way you can't manufacture."

He stopped, thinking, and I waited as what he'd just said sunk in.

"Oh," he said. "It was *authentic.* I was being authentic, and it sparked authenticity in everyone else. That's why that moment connected us so much."

Over the next several months, as the lockdown dragged on, Nathan began to seek out more opportunities for authentic connection through the screen. He always started with the question I'd asked him: "What makes you *you?*" (This actually became an icebreaker in one of the pre-meeting breakout sessions he arranged.)

He found that, contrary to what he'd initially thought, there were actually a multitude of opportunities for connection that he'd never considered in the office environment. In many ways, his team being remote only served to strengthen Nathan's understanding of how to create deep, lasting relationships with his team members, and how to keep the team connected—even across the digital divide.

As the leader, the authenticity that will unite your team begins with you.

How can you reveal your truest self to your team?

What makes you *you?*

Answering these questions is the beginning of a long investment, one that yields huge returns in true connection, and ultimately, a brilliantly connected, brilliantly performing team.

YOU GET SOLID: SELF-EVALUATION

1. What makes you *you*?

2. When do you feel your most authentic at work? Is there a specific experience or moment you can point to where you fully brought your whole self? Conversely, can you think of a time when you didn't feel like your authentic self, or that your authenticity was in conflict with your environment?

3. What challenges in your work connections have you encountered in our evolving work landscape? What opportunities?

4. Do you feel you have authentic connections at work? In your life? With your peers, your manager, your team members?

THEY GET SOLID: NEXT STEPS

1. Ask for volunteers to sign in to the next team video call ten minutes early to facilitate some "magic in the moments." Build this as a practice with any remote meet-ings—or set aside a few minutes at the beginning of team meetings to create some magic.

2. Have each team member reflect on the moments they feel most authentic. Brainstorm ways each person can bring their unique authenticity into the workday.

5

BRILLIANCE

Gallup research shows employees who know and use their strengths are six times as likely to be engaged at work, nearly eight times more productive in their role, and much less likely overall to leave their company.[55]

"Do I *like* my job...or am I just great at it?"

Over the years, as I've worked with hundreds of hypertalented, super driven executives and leaders, I've come to notice that they often have a different level of measurement when it comes to their performance. Being great at one's job would seem like a high water mark to most people. For some clients I coach, it's more like sea level.

I had been working with Darius, a sales executive at a large telecommunications company, for just over three months. In that time, I'd come to know him as an extremely intelligent, thoughtful, and people-focused leader. He was also deeply driven by accomplishment, always reaching for the next goal, crushing it, and coming up with a new bar to clear. We'll talk in a later

---

55 Peter Flade, Jim Asplund, and Gwen Elliot, "Employees Who Use Their Strengths Outperform Those Who Don't," Gallup, October 8, 2015, https://www.gallup.com/workplace/236561/employees-strengths-outperform-don.aspx.

chapter about the practice of "getting stretchy"—continually inhabiting the space just beyond your comfort zone for accelerated growth—and Darius is one of the "stretchiest" individuals I've worked with.

But almost immediately when we began our sessions, something began to emerge that had been quietly lurking under the surface of Darius's drive and accomplishments.

He didn't love his work.

He wasn't passionate about *what* he was doing, only that he did it to the best of his ability.

Darius had been feeling a sense of listlessness for about a year before he sought out my coaching. Despite how hard he pushed himself on his goals, and despite the way he blew the expectations of his role out of the water, he was ending his days dissatisfied.

"I used to feel good when I got another gold star from our CEO, or when our team hit another huge milestone. But even those accomplishments aren't doing anything for me anymore," he told me. "I'm happy to have achieved them, obviously, and I don't want to sound ungrateful, but... something's missing."

He shrugged. "I just don't feel the hustle, the fire, that I used to feel. I'm beginning to dread going to work. And at this point, so many people rely on me—I don't want to let them down. But I'm starting to wonder...is this even what I want to be doing?"

Darius had begun to identify something many of my clients have struggled with: being *good* at something isn't the same thing as *liking* it.

Our society tends to place a high premium on status, accomplishment, and praise—and it starts when we're young. Raise your hand if you were ever deemed an "overachiever" as a kid (hi, me too!). Many of us are trained from a young age to chase after those gold stars, tick off the next goal, never stop moving, driving, pushing toward the next big win.

In all that pressure and drive, it's easy to mix up the high we feel from getting the wins with the actual spark of joy that comes with doing something we truly love and are passionate about. And often—as I've experienced with many of my clients—we're so busy climbing the ladder faster and faster that, when we get to the top, we might look around and realize suddenly, *uh oh—do I actually love this view?*

As a leader, you may have noticed this phenomenon in the people you lead as well. Another client of mine, Amy, recently told me a story about one of her top team members, Katie. Katie was young, highly ambitious, and a monster achiever. She'd come into the organization like a whirlwind and made a huge impression, rising very quickly in the ranks. Within six months, the higher-ups in the company were considering Katie for a VP role in another division.

Amy told me that this news had sent Katie into an emotional spiral. "She was a bit of a basket case for a week," Amy said. "She wanted so badly to be excited about the promotion and making VP, but I could tell she was freaking out. There was some part of her deep down that was screaming, *Hit the brakes!* And the rest of her was screaming, *Why? This is what we've been working for!*"

When Amy finally sat Katie down to sort out how Katie *really* felt about the promotion, Katie had gotten a little teary. "I honestly just love our team, and I love working with you and being mentored by you. But I know I'll probably like it over there just as much. I know I'll be great in the role."

It took a lot of unpacking, but Amy helped Katie see that she was mixing up *talent* and *passion*. "Katie, you're incredibly talented. That's why you're here. You'd be great at *most* things," Amy had said. "Have you ever thought about not just what you're good at, but what you *like?"*

Katie had been confused. "But what if what I like isn't what I'm good *at?"*

"First, I'll repeat: *you'd be good at most things.* And second, you're saying right now that what you like is being on this team and working with me. Would you agree that you're great in your current role, doing just that?"

Katie had nodded, and, as Amy put it to me later, "I watched the light dawn on her face. She'd truly never considered that, with enough talent to have her pick of jobs, she could actually put the priority on doing what she loved most. And by staying in her role, she's also leaning into a longer professional growth curve that will end up with her in an even higher leadership position down the road."

I've referred to the spark you have the opportunity to ignite in every member of your team, the spark that comes from deep within you and ripples throughout everyone you touch.

What does that spark look like?

You probably know what it *feels* like: that wonderful glow of doing work you love, being in flow, ending the day energized and feeling great about what you accomplished. The spark is in those moments when you don't even notice the time passing, and what you're doing no longer feels like work. The deep enjoyment and satisfaction of your work cause time to fly past—you look up as the sky begins to darken and think, *yikes! It's already dinnertime?*

As a leader, finding your spark and focusing as much time and energy into that place where you're uniquely passionate and productive is of paramount importance. The spark of each of your team members begins with you—and by finding yours, you can help them find theirs too.

WHAT MAKES YOU BRILLIANT?

Right off the bat, I'll bet you're wondering: why do you need to *find* your spark? Isn't it obvious?

Well, no. Not always. In fact, it often takes some detective work.

First of all, research has shown that two-thirds of people have no meaningful awareness of what their true strengths are.[56] If that's you, you're in good company, and that's probably a sign to start looking.

Have you ever taken a strengths assessment? I have. Dozens of them, actually. They're useful in that you're able to quickly get a glance at where you should be focusing your efforts to maximize productivity and results.

However, they're not much help in maximizing *happiness*.

---

56 Dr. Ryan Niemiec, "What Are Your Signature Strengths?" VIA Institute on Character, March 23, 2012, https://www.viacharacter.org/topics/articles/what-are-your-signature-strengths.

It's one thing to know your strengths, but your greatest potential—the furthest reaches of your positive number line—lies in the strengths that *energize* you. Your greatest potential lies not just in your talents, but in your unique brilliance.

Cultivating and activating your unique strengths is a key practice of Positive Psychology. The VIA Institute on Character, founded by Positive Psychology researcher Dr. Neal Mayerson, funded a team of fifty-five social scientists to study world cultures, philosophies, and psychology to identify core human virtues—the traits associated with the positive end of the number line. Led by Dr. Martin Seligman and Dr. Christopher Peterson, this team crafted a list of twenty-four positive human traits that spans all cultures, nationalities, and time periods. They consider each individual's top character strengths to be defined by three key elements:[57]

1. **Essential:** The strength feels essential to who you are as a person.

2. **Effortless:** When you use the strength, it feels natural and effortless.

3. **Energizing:** Using the strength energizes and uplifts you. It leaves you feeling happy, in balance, and ready to take on more.

When I work with clients who are trying to uncover their spark, I continually bring them back to these three elements. I ask them to notice how they feel doing different types of work, and to ask themselves: *Does this feel essential? Effortless? Energizing?*

---

57 Peterson and Seligman, *Character Strengths and Virtues*.

Studies show that when employees do work that they're passionate about, performance skyrockets. Employees focusing deeply on their strengths are nearly 8 percent more productive; and teams that discuss their strengths every day are 12.5 percent more productive.[58] Companies that invest in the unique talents of their employees enjoy higher profitability and greater earnings per share. Sales go up. Customer engagement climbs, and more employees feel an emotional connection to their workplace.

And yet, despite all the above benefits of intentionally guiding employees toward work that truly fires them up, studies also show that this isn't the norm in our current workplace culture. In 2019, a Deloitte survey reported that only 20 percent of employees feel "truly passionate" about their work, and close to 70 percent of the workforce is "actively disengaged."[59]

Feeling fulfilled, engaged, energized, and valuable in the work that you do are key indicators of happiness in the workplace. And employee happiness? That's where the greatest potential for performance lies. A study by the University of Warwick showed that employees who reported higher levels of happiness were 12 percent more productive overall than employees who reported unhappiness or disengagement.[60] Furthermore, unhappiness actually had a detrimental effect on productivity—the level dipped below baseline productivity in individuals who reported that they were unhappy in their jobs.

---

58 Susan Sorenson, "How Employees' Strengths Make Your Company Stronger," Gallup, February 20, 2014, https://news.gallup.com/businessjournal/167462/employees-strengths-company-stronger.aspx.

59 Drea Zigarmi and Randy Conley, "Focus on Employee Work Passion, Not Employee Engagement," Workforce.com, March 14, 2019, https://workforce.com/news/focus-employee-work-passion-employee-engagement.

60 Jonha Revesencio, "Why Happy Employees Are 12% More Productive," *Fast Company*, July 22, 2015, https://www.fastcompany.com/3048751/happy-employees-are-12-more-productive-at-work.

Happier employees show greater company loyalty, higher levels of engagement and advocacy, and increased motivation. Most importantly, employee happiness is correlated with *leader* happiness. A study of 357 leaders showed that those who were deeply fulfilled and happy in their work, and who led with a positive mood, were more likely to be viewed by employees as transformational.[61]

If you can locate and focus on the work that makes you *most* fulfilled—the precise intersection of your greatest strengths and your biggest passions—your performance can soar. And because the spark begins with you, the performance of your team will take flight right alongside you.

Strengths in Numbers

- According to Gallup, simply learning their strengths makes employees 7.8 percent more productive, and teams that focus on strengths every day have 12.5 percent greater productivity.[62]

- Strengths-based development leads to 19 percent increased sales, 29 percent increased profit, 7 percent higher customer engagement, and a 15 percent increase in engaged employees.[63]

---

61 Helena Vieira, "Do Happy People Lead Better?" LSE Business Review, July 12, 2016, https://blogs.lse.ac.uk/businessreview/2016/07/12/do-happy-people-lead-better/.

62 Sorenson, "How Employees' Strengths."

63 Brandon Rigoni and Jim Asplund, "Strengths-Based Employee Development: The Business Results," Gallup, July 7, 2016, https://www.gallup.com/workplace/236297/strengths-based-employee-development-business-results.aspx.

- Business leaders who invest in building cultures where people are positioned to do what they do best every day see up to 59 percent fewer safety incidents and 72 percent lower turnover.[64]

MY BIG SPARK

From the time I was a little girl, I've always been fascinated by people—how they act, react, and interact. Throughout my school years, I took advantage of any opportunity I could find to study psychology, and eventually, at Duke, majored in the field. I loved *everything* about psychology. I was never bored.

But then, my senior year of college, companies came to campus to recruit for the next year—and I got waylaid one day by an investment banking firm who painted me a glamorous picture of New York finance life. At that age, when we're all at the beginning of building our lives and we're hungry to feel accomplished and respectable, banking seemed like something I "should" do, the kind of career I'd be an idiot to turn down. So I interviewed, got a job at an investment firm, and moved to NYC.

This is where, in an 80s movie montage, you'd see twenty-two-year-old Jackie excitedly imagining herself sitting down in conference rooms and dramatically counting her stacks of cash…and then screen wipe to scenes of stark reality, where she's chained to a dreary cubicle, eating crappy

---

64 Rigoni and Asplund, "Strengths-Based Employee Development."

takeout for every meal, crashing into bed in her tiny hole of an apartment at an ungodly time each night, barely kicking off her shoes in her exhaustion. Yeah. It was all of three months before I realized I'd made a mistake. I'm generally *very* quick to notice when I'm miserable, and boy, did that job make me miserable.

One day while rushing to a corner deli down the street during the fifteen minutes I had for lunch, I caught a glimpse of myself in a shop window and stopped dead. I looked tired, defeated, totally *done*.

Right there on the street, I burst into tears. I stood sobbing despondently into my hands, the busy city around me taking absolutely *no* notice. (That's not a movie cliché—New Yorkers are pretty accustomed to people having breakdowns in public. Just another Tuesday in the Big Apple.)

What am I doing? I asked myself. *This isn't what I wanted.*

Was I good at the job? Yes. Absolutely. I was good with numbers, I could do math, and I was a hard worker.

Was I happy? Was I fulfilled? *Hell no.* Day in and day out, I sat behind a desk by myself for fourteen hours crunching numbers in spreadsheets. It was somehow mind-numbing and stressful at the same time. I didn't have any work friends; I didn't even have time to try to make any, with my blink-and-you'll-miss-it lunch break. It was just me and Excel in a numbers battle from sunup to sundown. I was in my apartment for so little time each day that I couldn't keep a plant alive, let alone relax or try to have a social life. The only other person I ever saw outside of work was my roommate, in passing, as we squeezed by each other in and out of our tiny windowless bathroom.

Standing there sobbing in the busiest city in the world, people bumping and elbowing me as they passed, I'd never felt so alone.

Until another New Yorker actually reached out with compassion.

It was Fred, the man who camped in front of the corner deli and could often be found hanging out on the front steps of our office building. Fred came up next to me and put his arm around my shoulders. Any other day, I'd probably have been freaked out at a stranger initiating physical contact in the middle of the sidewalk. But as lonely and hopeless as I felt, I didn't shrink away from Fred.

He patted my shoulder and said simply, "It's gonna be okay."

It's amazing how the smallest moments can sometimes make the biggest impact. That was a life-changing moment for me. It was the moment I realized that my life, my career, my current predicament with what I'd found to be a soul-sucking job, and even the emotional state I was in were all *choices.*

This is a choice, I thought. *I have a choice. I get to decide what happens next.*

"Thank you," I said shakily to Fred, then turned around, went upstairs to the office, and quit on the spot.

It was hasty, and probably an irrational move, because I didn't have another job lined up or even any prospects. But I was suddenly so clear on what I had to do. I had to make a choice to go after happiness. I had to choose fulfillment. I had to find my spark, the livelihood that I was not just good at, but that also energized me.

I was great at my job. But I didn't *like* it.

My boss at the firm (who hated me anyway) nodded as though she wasn't surprised, gave me a cursory "We'll mail you your last check; good luck," and that was it. I was out.

I went back downstairs into the sunny afternoon, wiping tear tracks from my face and smiling for the first time in weeks. Fred had moved on to another block, perhaps to drop some wisdom on another sobbing young person who was questioning their life choices. I walked home to the apartment I could no longer afford feeling lighter than air.

From there, I'd like to say I immediately found my passion, the career that lit my spark, but it wasn't as straightforward as that—the line was pretty squiggly throughout the rest of my twenties as it led me to graduate school at Harvard, then to Tickle.com writing online quizzes, and then deeper and deeper into the realm of Positive Psychology and human behavior. Through it all, though, I was led by a new determination. I was going to find my spark. I was going to prioritize happiness, fulfillment, being lit from within by the work I was doing. As long as I followed that drive, I couldn't go wrong.

RANDOM PATTERNS OF LIGHT

When I think of what makes a sparkler beautiful, I think of the randomness and unpredictability of the sparks.

Your eyes don't know where the next bright shimmer is going to come from—it's just a cloud of glowy sparkle shooting off in all directions. Each spark is unique in its size, shape, and trajectory. Together, they create the full effect.

This is also how I think of teams of people working together. The most effective teams, the teams that create incredible change and drive the most results, are the teams that include many different sparks harmonizing into a fiery light show.

As a leader, your role is to guide and nurture the natural spark not only within yourself, but within each person you lead. This will also organically strengthen the performance of your team—to get the absolute best out of each of them individually and as a group.

As we've discussed, people often have trouble discerning between their *strengths* and their *spark*. Helping each person focus on and leverage their greatest source of brilliance ensures that your team has the diversity of thought, insight, talent, and passion to create the largest field of impact possible.

Key Concept: Cognitive Diversity

The more diversity of thought and perspective your team has, the stronger it is. And the more you, the leader, can promote the discovery of each individual's unique perspective, the greater power you have to meet people where they are and create an emotional climate of safety and trust. Double bonus.

Put more simply, more perspectives equal better decisions and a more positive culture.

One study found that when leaders leverage the unique skills and capabilities of their employees, productivity and operating margins increase by fifty percent.[65] Another study[66] by the *Harvard Business Review* measured the level of cognitive diversity across six teams undertaking the same exercise. The results showed a high positive correlation of cognitive diversity and performance, with the three more-diverse teams performing over 100 percent better than teams that had more homogenous knowledge processing and perspective.

As a leader, you want to nourish cognitive diversity by teasing out the unique lens and contribution each person you lead brings to a situation. By taking the time to discover each unique perspective and bring them into your own perspective as the leader, you're able to achieve comprehensive knowledge and make better decisions. Moreover, the team is able to work faster, produce more, and accelerate learning in complex situations.

Promoting cognitive diversity begins with you—your commitment to outlook, mindset, and connection with each individual. The Platinum Rule is nowhere more evident than in a team with high cognitive diversity. By taking the time to discover each person's unique perspective and meeting them where they want to be met, it's possible to leverage far more from each person, and in turn, leverage far more from the team.

---

65 Michael Mankins, "Great Companies Obsess Over Productivity, Not Efficiency," *Harvard Business Review*, March 1, 2017, https://hbr.org/2017/03/great-companies-obsess-over-productivity-not-efficiency.

66 Alison Reynolds and David Lewis, "Teams Solve Problems Faster When They're More Cognitively Diverse," *Harvard Business Review*, March 30, 2017, https://hbr.org/2017/03/teams-solve-problems-faster-when-theyre-more-cognitively-diverse.

PLAN OF ACTION

Helping your team uncover and focus on their individual sparks can be so powerful that it's worth making it a strategic priority. Here's your action plan.

Action #1: Project Reflection

After the culmination of a project, ask each team member a series of questions to reflect on how it went—with a focus on their own connection to the work.

1. What about this energized you the most?

2. What drained you?

3. Where do you think you did your best work?

4. When did time seem to just fly by?

5. What frustrated you?

Keep pulling at the threads and see what emerges. For example, you'll learn right away which team members enjoy working with the fine details of a project, and which are enthralled by creating visions and generating ideas. And once you get the lay of the land, you can start digging a little deeper.

What do you like about immersing yourself in the details?

What do you like about brainstorming?

If you could have spent the whole project focused on one aspect, which one would have fired you up the most?

You'll uncover opportunities that suit each individual's preferences and find ways to put them in a position to stretch those muscles in the future.

Action #2: Calendar Audit

Next, walk your team through a calendar audit, then set it as a regular practice. The first step in starting to identify what energizes you and what drains you is simply noticing your physical reactions to what's coming up on your calendar.

Instruct your team members to scan their calendars on a weekly basis. When they look at the week ahead, what makes them think, *yay! Can't wait!* and what gives them an "ugh" feeling in their stomach? There's also a neutral reaction that's totally valid—events that they neither look forward to nor dread. Have them color code their calendar events: grey or brown for the "ugh" items, a neutral beige or pale blue for the neutral ones, and a bright happy color (I like to simply use my favorite color) for the "yay" items.

Then, ask them to dig deeper with these questions:

1. What do these energizing events have in common?

2. What is it about them that gets you excited?

3. What are some themes in the events you find yourself dreading?

Over the course of a few weeks, you'll start to see a few trends emerge. It's a great way for team members to more consciously break down what kind of things energize and uplift their energy, and which ones feel more depleting. They might find they truly love working with the people from advertising or manufacturing, or it could be they like meeting with potential business partners because it's an opportunity to learn more about related industries. It may become clear to them that not only do they have a knack for making connections between different divisions of the company, but that the process of doing so feels especially rewarding.

Action #3: The X-O Exercise

Once team members become more aware of what energizes them, the next logical step is to help them figure out how they can bring more of that into their day-to-day working life. This is where I recommend the X-O Exercise.

Start with a blank sheet of paper with a big O drawn at the top, a big X at the bottom, and a line drawn horizontally through the middle to divide the paper into two halves.

Keep this next to you on your desk all day for a couple of weeks. This isn't going to add extra time to your day—you're simply going to notice how you feel about your work in the moment and capture that feeling on the X-O sheet.

Whenever you're working on tasks that are your core responsibilities— your "must-dos," that only you can do—write them *inside* the O. And when you're working on things that fire you up and light your spark— not necessarily a core responsibility, but something you love and want to keep on your plate—write them *outside* the O, above the line.

But when you're doing a task or a type of work that *totally* doesn't fire you up—the kind of stuff that annoys you or makes your gut go *ugh*— write it down in the X area of the sheet, below the line. These could also be tasks that aren't the best use of your time, that someone else on the team could do, or could learn to do.

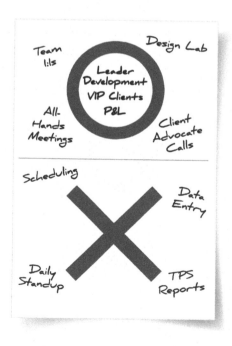

After a week or two of jotting these down in their appropriate sections, you'll have a clear visual representation of how you feel about your work in general. Everything that ends up above the line, either inside or outside the O, is work you want to focus on and where you want to spend more time. Everything below the X is work you want to get off your plate, period.

Here's the wonderful thing about what's in the X area: your X might be someone else's O!

This happens often when I work with teams; I'll have them all complete the X-O exercise, and when they're done, everyone shares their Xs. Frequently, someone else will raise their hand and say, "You *don't* like doing that task/project/what have you? I would *love* to do that!" Time for a swap!

For you, as the leader, everything below the X represents an opportunity to delegate, to scope out a hire that may be needed, or to teach your team members a new responsibility. What represents an X for you might be an incredible opportunity to start a new growth path for one of your employees.

I recently guided a few clients through this exercise. Martina, Susan, and Cassandra had founded a marketing agency together, and their business was soon growing so quickly that they'd never really slowed down to reflect on their unique strengths and passions.

When they completed the X-O Exercise, we found that, despite their similar backgrounds in marketing, each partner had listed different energizing strengths on the X-O sheet. As it turned out, Cassandra's spark was in business development; she loved the networking aspect and the high-level dealmaking. Martina's was client management. She loved building relationships with their clients, and couldn't wait to get on the phone with each one to diagnose how best to help grow their business. Susan, in contrast, preferred to talk to clients as little as possible—which surprised everyone, considering she'd been highly successful in account management throughout her career. Susan's spark was on the creative side, developing strategic marketing assets. Each partner had a unique passion that had the potential to skyrocket the business even more if they were freed up enough to focus on it.

The bottom of the chart was the exact *opposite*. They had all listed exactly the same things. All of them hated billing, scheduling, making travel plans, returning phone calls, filing, preparing invoices, and admin duties.

Their course of action became immediately clear: first, hire an executive assistant, and second, outsource their billing.

Within just one month of taking action, their business went from "skyrocketing" to "lightspeed." The simple step of focusing their time and energy on the work they were most passionate about and fulfilled by was a total game changer.

BUSINESS BREAKTHROUGHS

As a business leader, you definitely want your employees working in flow in their area of greatest talent and passion. Employees who are disengaged from the work they're doing cost the US economy $450 billion to $500 billion annually.[67] A Deloitte study showed that only 13 percent of employees are passionate about their jobs—that's 87 percent of employees who haven't found their spark! Employees who have found their spark, meanwhile, measurably amplify outcomes for their companies. Seventy-one percent of passionate employees report working extra hours, and 68 percent report high optimism, which supports better collaboration and higher morale and productivity.[68]

LIMITLESS BRILLIANCE

When Darius began to realize that he'd been focusing too closely on his strengths, rather than the intersection of his strengths *and* passions, he became fully bought-in to discovering his spark. It was the next big goal for him to reach, the potential that lay beyond, as he put it, "mere greatness."

We began with a simple calendar audit. In identifying the parts of his week that he dreaded, and the parts he was most excited about, a common thread emerged: more than anything, Darius was fired up when he got to help *other people* achieve greatness.

---

67   Susan Sorenson and Keri Garman, "How to Tackle U.S. Employees' Stagnating Engagement," Gallup, June 11, 2013, https://news.gallup.com/businessjournal/162953/tackle-employees-stagnating-engagement.aspx.

68   "Deloitte Study: Only 13 Percent of the US Workforce Is Passionate About Their Jobs," Cision PRNewswire, June 7, 2017, https://www.prnewswire.com/news-releases/deloitte-study-only-13-percent-of-the-us-workforce-is-passionate-about-their-jobs-300469952.html.

"It's all the conversations I have with people outside my core responsibilities," he explained to me. "It's the meetings that usually begin with people asking, 'Hey, can I pick your brain?' It's all the mentoring, guiding, and teaching I do that I've always considered 'on the side,' but that I'm now seeing *really* moves the needle not only for those people, but for the company."

Building connections with employees throughout the organization and coaching them toward their potential wasn't explicitly in his job description, but it turned out that it was what he loved most. Being a coach brought him tremendous satisfaction in a way no other work ever had (I can relate!). And the kicker—he'd never received a single gold star, promotion, or salary bump for doing that work. It was something he loved without needing to be outright celebrated for it.

Darius began a "side adventure" in his career, one that kept him strong in the hustle, drive, and goal-crushing that had led to his success, but that also incorporated the spark he'd recently discovered. He created a mentorship program at the company that developed future leaders and paired them with champions that would help them grow and develop internally. Today, he's a key leader in the business resource group at his company that focuses on employee mentorship.

"I never would have seen myself here five years ago," he told me recently on a catch-up call. "And I'm the happiest I've ever been."

And as for crushing goals? In the two years Darius has been participating in mentorship, the company has seen double-digit increases in employee engagement and retention. Recently, they made the list of the best places to work in their state for the first time…and cracked the top twenty.

Great leaders develop strengths. *Exceptional* leaders develop sparks.

YOU GET SOLID: SELF-EVALUATION

1. Perform your own calendar audit. What upcoming events are you most excited about?

2. Are there any events on your calendar you're dreading? Why?

3. If you could spend your whole day just doing one thing, and finish completely energized, what would that one thing be?

4. Create your X-O sheet and fill it out over the course of two weeks. Then evaluate: what should you get off your plate? Are there any stretch opportunities for your team members?

THEY GET SOLID: NEXT STEPS

1. Ask each team member to perform a calendar audit, and work with each to identify the upcoming work they're most and least passionate about.

2. Conduct a roundtable where each team member gives their assessment of *other* team members' sparks. Seeing

themselves reflected in their teammates' perspectives can be a powerful eye-opener.

3. Schedule project reflections on a regular cadence that assess not just the success of the project, but how each team member felt about it—what lit them up the most, and how can you guide their role to focus them more on that passion?

6

TRUST

A 2019 HBR Survey found that 58 percent of employees trust a complete stranger more than their own boss.[69]

"Can you stop by my office in an hour? I have some feedback for you."

Awesome! Can't wait!

…thought no one, ever.

Eric stared at the Slack message from his boss, Marcus, which had just flown in from the right side of his screen. The friendly chirp of the little notification box belied its contents. Eric's stomach immediately dropped, and he felt his palms get sweaty.

Yikes. Feedback? What feedback? What did I do wrong this time?

Marcus led the marketing department at the company, a team of twenty-five. Most of the time, he was a gregarious and fun boss, always ready

---

69   Sebastian Martinez, "58% of Employees Trust a Stranger More than Their Boss," LinkedIn, January 27, 2021, https://www.linkedin.com/pulse/58-employees-trust-stranger-more-than-boss-sebastian-martinez?trk=pulse-article_more-articles_related-content-card.

with a joke or a hilarious anecdote. He dropped pop culture references like a flower girl flinging rose petals at a wedding, adding color to even the driest meetings at their midsize SaaS company. He had an encyclopedic knowledge of seemingly every meme and GIF on the internet and lit the team's Slack channels up with well-timed uses—impressive for a forty-eight-year-old father of three who thought TikTok was a spicy corn chip.

He was also a great teacher and coach, able to guide individual team members through friction points into higher and higher levels of knowledge and ability. From the outside, he seemed like exactly the kind of boss you'd want to grow your career with.

The only problem? He could be *too* intense, and his intensity was totally unpredictable.

His employees never knew if they were going to get fun-happy-times Marcus, or the *other* Marcus—the one who would sting with quick, cutting criticism, then follow it with a smile and a joke. Some meetings were full of levity and laughter, and some became long rabbit holes centered around whatever mistake or misstep Marcus felt the team had made. He had a way of striking when they least expected it; he could be mid-grin and then suddenly shift to intense coaching mode, like a freak storm blowing in, blotting out the sun.

If a team member didn't know the answer to a question, Marcus went in on them in front of the group—always *just* jokingly enough that it could be construed as constructive, but that left the person in the hot seat self-conscious and anxious. If something wasn't prepared exactly the way he had expected it, Marcus spent everyone's time in a meeting singling out the person who had prepared it, taking them through exactly what they had done wrong and how to do it next time. He liked to use what he called the "Socratic method" in meetings, but from Eric's perspective, that meant little more than putting people on the spot, then inundating them with coaching when they stumbled nervously over an answer they hadn't really had time to think about.

Everyone on the team existed tensely on a high wire of anticipation, waiting for the inevitable out-of-the-blue Slack message from Marcus taking apart something they'd done, or asking them to put coaching time on the calendar with him, offering no specifics.

And it wasn't that his criticisms—*feedback,* as he liked to call it—were even off-base. He was completely right almost one hundred percent of the time. When he wasn't right, he did listen to see where he'd made the wrong assumption, or get to the bottom of what he hadn't understood. He wasn't unreasonable. His "feedback" *did* serve his employees in becoming better and more effective at their work.

The problem wasn't the content. It was the delivery.

Marcus was a frequent topic of conversation during my sessions with Eric, with whom I'd been working for six months.

"I really do appreciate getting to work with him. I honestly think he's inspired more personal and professional growth in me than almost anyone else in my entire career," Eric told me on a Friday afternoon video call. "He's incredibly smart and generous with his time and energy. But I'm also walking on eggshells. He's like a grenade with the pin pulled—I never know when he's going to go off."

I asked him what would feel more stable. "What would it look like and feel like to know where you stand with Marcus?"

Eric paused to think. "I don't really know," he finally said. "But what it feels like right now is the constant stress of waiting for the hammer to drop. I can tell it's affecting my work and my relationship with Marcus. What it feels like now is…fear, honestly. I'm in a constant low simmer of fear."

What flashed through my mind immediately was Yoda dropping wisdom from atop a rock in the mists of Dagobah: *Fear is the path to the dark side.*

Eric was quickly reaching the end of his rope. I suspected the rest of the team felt the same way. And as long as the team felt such a low sense of safety, they were bound to reach a breaking point.

SAFETY FIRST

The whole is greater than the sum of its parts.

Aristotle knew what he was talking about (even if, truthfully, the above adage is a common re-interpretation of his original quote). A team working together in flow, shared energy, common purpose, and aligned motivation is always more effective than each single team member, no matter how excellent they may be.

Leaders know this, and as a leader, you know that creating an environment where the team can get to that state is your driving purpose.

But how do you get your team to reach their collective potential? How do you know when your team is operating at peak performance?

A few years ago, Google set out to answer this question through a study called Project Aristotle, which was designed to determine why some teams excelled while others did not. Their examination of more than 180 teams from around the world revealed something unexpected: the traits and performance of individuals on a team matter less than how the team members interact, structure their work, and view their contributions. It's the group norms that matter—the traditions, behavioral practices, and unwritten rules that shape how teams work together.[70]

Project Aristotle researchers concluded that the best teams exhibit five qualities:

1. **Dependability.** People on the team do what they say they'll do, and they do it on time.

2. **Structure and clarity.** The team knows its goal and each member has a well-defined role in achieving that.

3. **Meaning.** Each team member feels their work has personal significance.

4. **Impact.** The group feels their work will serve the greater good.

5. **Psychological safety.** Team members feel safe taking risks, stating opinions, and asking questions without fear of being judged. Team members feel free to let down their guard and say what they mean.[71]

---

70 Gary Burnison, "7 Years Ago, Google Set Out to Find What Makes the 'Perfect' Team—and What They Found Shocked Other Researchers," CNBC.com, September 13, 2019, https://www.cnbc.com/2019/02/28/what-google-learned-in-its-quest-to-build-the-perfect-team.html.

71 Ibid.

Google found that this last quality, *psychological safety*, was far and away the most important indicator of a team's success. Employees who worked in a psychologically safe environment were less likely to leave the company, eager to enjoy the benefits of diversity, and more successful across the board using a variety of measures. Those who felt psychologically safe felt free to take risks and ask questions. They didn't worry about seeming ignorant, incompetent, or unprepared. They were confident that no one on the team would embarrass or punish them for admitting a mistake.

In other words, they were working in the exact *opposite* of the environment Marcus had created.

For leaders, the challenge is clear: how can you establish an environment in which people can thrive? How can you create a workplace where people aren't afraid to raise their hands and share their thoughts without being judged? Where people can listen without judging their colleagues? Where people can shine, take risks, and learn?

These intangible qualities form a sort of magnetic field that draws people in and bonds them together. They create an environment where people feel supported and safe in not just their work, but also in their professional and personal growth. Safety is a feeling beyond our primary instinct for survival, which so often occupies our subconscious. When you're seeing the bear, all you're thinking about is the bear. Only when you're completely certain that the bear isn't going to jump out at you from behind a tree can you think about anything beyond getting to safety. Once you're safe, you can begin to think and live into your full potential.

In this sense, psychological safety is not about protecting people from risk, but instead about creating an environment where people feel safe enough to *take* risks—and take accountability. Psychological safety isn't about treating your employees like they're fragile little eggshells that need to be rolled up and protected in bubble wrap.

Quite the opposite: it's about *encouraging courage*.

Courage is a function of trust. Courageous employees who volunteer vulnerability, take risks, and stretch beyond their comfort zone *trust* their team, their workplace, and their leader. They trust that they won't be judged, berated, or abandoned. They trust that their *belongingness* is secure, no matter what stumbles they make or what growth they're in the middle of.

As a leader, building trust is your focus.

TRUST DOESN'T HAPPEN BY ACCIDENT

Trust in leadership is one of the strongest indicators of a high-performing, engaged organization. Study after study shows that when employees don't trust their leaders, their productivity, happiness, and commitment to the company plummet, and their likelihood of looking elsewhere for employment rises precipitously.

Examples of CEOs who are *not* trusted by their teams and companies are rampant, from that friend in your spin class who's always ranting about their "psycho" boss (not an idle complaint—according to experts, anywhere from four to twelve percent of CEOs exhibit psychopathic traits[72]) to news stories about C-suite misdeeds, to film and television (when it comes to spine-chilling evil, Meryl Streep in *The Devil Wears*

---

72 Jack McCullough, "The Psychopathic CEO," *Forbes*, December 9, 2019, https://www.forbes.com/sites/jackmccullough/2019/12/09/the-psychopathic-ceo/?sh=574d920f791e.

Prada ranks right up there with Darth Vader for me—and come to think of it, Vader didn't exactly promote trust amongst his employees, either!).

A recent study by The Ken Blanchard Companies measured the impact that leader trustworthiness has on employee engagement. The results showed an enormous and consistent correlation between employees' sense of trust and their intent to perform well, go above and beyond, stay with the business, and be an advocate for the company. More importantly, employee trust was a direct result of specific coaching behaviors undertaken by leaders.[73]

Trust doesn't happen by accident. As a leader, you have the ability to directly create and impact trust with your team members. It begins with you, and like all other aspects of Platinum Leadership, psychological safety is a direct result of your actions, practices, and communication as a leader.

Safety in Numbers

- Ninety-eight percent of workers say their performance improves when they feel confident at work.[74]

- Compared with people at low-trust companies, people at high-trust companies report: 74 percent less stress,

73 David Witt, "Are Your Leaders Trustworthy? New Research Looks at the Impact of Coaching Behaviors," The Ken Blanchard Companies, January 12, 2017, https://resources.kenblanchard.com/blanchard-leaderchat/are-your-leaders-trustworthy-new-research-looks-at-the-impact-of-coaching-behaviors.

74 Liz Lewis, "Confidence at Work: Why Employers Should Nurture This Soft Skill," Indeed.com, January 23, 2020, https://www.indeed.com/lead/confidence-at-work.

106 percent more energy at work, 50 percent higher productivity, 13 percent fewer sick days, 76 percent more engagement, 29 percent more satisfaction with their lives, 40 percent less burnout.[75]

- A 2016 HOW Report concluded that employees who work in high-trust environments are thirty-two times more likely to take risks that might benefit the company, eleven times more likely to see higher levels of innovation relative to their competition, and six times more likely to achieve higher levels of performance compared with others in their industry.[76]

- Employees of organizations that don't actively work on creating a positive "psychosocial safety climate," where it's hard for employees to talk about mental health and seek support when they need it, are at three times greater risk of developing depression symptoms.[77]

---

75 Paul J. Zak, "The Neuroscience of Trust," *Harvard Business Review*, January 2017, https://hbr.org/2017/01/the-neuroscience-of-trust.

76 Michael Eichenwald and Susan Divers, "LRN's HOW Report: Outbehaving to Outperform," *Ethisphere*, https://magazine.ethisphere.com/lrns-how-report-outbehaving-to-outperform/.

77 University of South Australia, "Psychosocial Safety Climate: Toxic Workplaces Increase Risk of Depression by 300%," SciTechDaily, June 23, 2021, https://scitechdaily.com/psychosocial-safety-climate-toxic-workplaces-increase-risk-of-depression-by-300/.

> - Almost 100 (99.1) percent of employees prefer a workplace where people identify and discuss issues truthfully and effectively.[78]

THE TRUST ROADMAP

Building trust begins with *showing* trust.

Your best tool for creating psychological safety with your employees is to show them that you trust them—to model the safety and trust you want to create. The following practices are foundational to creating such an environment.

Action #1: Cultivate a Judgment-Free Zone

Let your team know in no uncertain terms that everyone is allowed to make mistakes, take risks, and offer thoughts and insights that are contrary to the popular opinion. In fact, take it one step further: *celebrate* mistakes as opportunities for learning and growth.

Cultivate a judgment-free zone in which everyone can ask questions that might sound stupid (but might ultimately be enlightening), and people are

---

78 Connie Certusi, "5 Leadership Lessons from Star Wars," The Business Journals, April 22, 2016, https://www.bizjournals.com/bizjournals/how-to/growth-strategies/2016/04/5-leadership-lessons-from-star-wars.html.

comfortable admitting that they don't understand something, even when they might feel like they should.

The quickest way to convey all of this is to model it yourself. Intentionally seek out genuine opportunities to admit you don't know something, and ask "the dumb questions." Showing your team members that you don't fear judgment goes a long way to prompting the same belief in them.

Additionally, lean into curious communication; ask questions and seek to understand the opinions and motivations of your team members, especially when they're bringing an opposing opinion to the table.

Excising judgment from your work environment eradicates shame, which heads off fear before it can even begin to flicker. It also creates an atmosphere in which people feel safe enough to take risks.

Action #2: Share Your Mistakes

A quick scroll of your LinkedIn feed probably shows dozens of posts and articles from business leaders sharing nuggets like "The Top Five Best _____" and "The Most Successful Ways I _____."

Sharing your successes can be a useful teaching tool, to be sure—but when it comes to building trust with your team, sharing your *failures* can be even more impactful. As humans and professionals, our "highlight reel" isn't the whole story, and it's not what makes us who we are; our brilliance often shines most brightly in the challenges we overcame and grew from most.

Employees who see their leader reflecting on their mistakes, and sharing them openly for the entire team to learn from immediately, sense that it's safe for them to share their own mistakes. Even more, it shows them that mistakes are natural and to be expected—and represent a great learning opportunity for everyone. A leader who shares their mistakes is an authentic leader, and a builder of authentic connection.

Action #3: Redefine Feedback

Eric's constant tension spiked whenever Marcus dropped that magic word on him: *feedback.*

Feedback is neither good nor bad. Feedback is simply a reflective response to action. It's also inherently colored by the lens of the person giving the feedback—it's subjective, not factual.

Yet in many workplaces, *feedback* has become synonymous with *criticism.*

You have the power to redefine your team's relationship with the word and create a true feedback-driven culture.

What this looks like is simple: find opportunities to give positive feedback, and begin to tie the word with positivity. This isn't necessarily because we want to create a wholly positive connotation with the word; rather, it's because the word is currently seen as *so* tied to the negative, we're going to lean into the positive harder to drag the word back to neutral. What we're going for is the word "feedback" having no negative or positive bias.

You can shift the emotional reaction your employees have to the word "feedback" by following the word with simple praise.

Can I give you some quick feedback? You did a great job on this.

You really nailed that presentation. My feedback: I'd like you to use it to create a presentation template to share with the team.

I got some feedback from the group you met with last week. They loved the clarity of your proposal and are excited to work with you on executing it.

The more you can tie the word "feedback" with positive emotions like pride, accomplishment, and satisfaction, the more you'll promote an environment where feedback isn't something to be feared, but something to be treated as a pure learning and growing opportunity.

This goes for you, too, as the leader: feedback is your food. Ask for feedback on your own performance as much as possible. Show your team members that you're hungry to know what they think of your leadership—what's serving them great, and what could serve them even better.

Executive coach Marshall Goldsmith has gone beyond redefining the word—he's completely rewritten it. Instead of *feedback,* he uses the term *feed forward.* In doing so, he first neutralizes any previous negative association with the word, then moves it into a realm of positive opportunity. The simple switch steers performance conversations toward growth and future success. When I use this approach with teams when sharing opportunities to improve, it lands so much easier without the defensive walls that so often naturally come up in response to feedback.

Action #4: Follow Through on Feedback

I hear a similar gripe from employees at all levels all the time:

I spoke up about something that was bothering me or that could be improved, and nothing happened.

Collecting feedback from employees only builds trust if they see that feedback reflected in your actions—if they see something *happen* as a result.

This doesn't mean that every piece of feedback you receive, every suggestion, complaint, or passing thought from team members, is immediately brought to fruition. Not all feedback is valid; not all ideas are good ones. As the leader, it's up to you to separate the wheat from the chaff.

But when employees share thoughts and ideas that are easily actionable and make sense for the organization, make it an imperative to follow through on them. Reward your team members for having the courage to speak up, take risks, and be honest.

Action #5: Promote Autonomy

Nothing shows an employee they're not trusted faster than micromanagement.

As a leader, it can sometimes be hard to allow your employees free rein on their work. Mistakes can set a whole team back significantly, and while they're obviously great learning opportunities, it would be better if they don't happen in the first place, right?

The only problem is that autonomy doesn't exist without mistakes. And employees who feel like their every move is being watched, managed, and tracked *know* deep down that their leaders don't trust them to execute.

Mistakes are going to happen. Show your team members that you trust them by allowing them the space to potentially make mistakes. By promoting autonomy—with, of course, the support and direction that makes autonomy effective—you'll create an environment where team members know that they're trusted to execute, and that if they make a mistake, they're trusted to fix it.

This is made especially powerful when expectations are clear and aligned from the beginning. When each team member knows the why and the context, has clarity around the goal and what the finished product will look like, and knows the importance of their role in the project—and when you help them prioritize and allow them consistent space for questions and reflection—the chance of costly mistakes is minimized. Autonomy doesn't have to come at the cost of higher error.

BUSINESS BREAKTHROUGHS

Low trust might just be the silent killer in many businesses. High-trust businesses have 50 percent less turnover than low-trust businesses.[79] Research shows that rebuilding trust once it's lost is five

---

79   Claire Hastwell, "The Business Returns on High-Trust Work Culture," GreatPlaceToWork.com, September 12, 2019, https://www.greatplacetowork.com/resources/blog/the-business-returns-on-high-trust-work-culture.

> times harder than creating that trust in the first place. And trust is a high marker for success—companies with cultures of high safety and trust showed a total return to shareholders that was *three times higher* across a three-year period.[80]

COURAGE TAKES TIME

The environment Marcus had created with his team wasn't going to be fixed in a day.

In fact, it ended up taking another six months for his employees to begin to feel psychologically safe.

At the time, I wasn't actually coaching Marcus—so guiding him on his own behavior wasn't an immediate option. Instead, I scheduled sessions with the entire team as a group, and even sat in on some of their team meetings.

My observations matched what I'd heard from Eric and a few other team members: Marcus was funny, brilliant, outgoing, generous with his time…and intense. His approach to coaching swung like a heavy pendulum between light guidance and "stop the meeting, everyone watch as I dissect this person's every opportunity for improvement." There wasn't

---

80 Aaron De Smet, Chris Gagnon, and Elizabeth Mygatt, "Organizing for the Future: Nine Keys to Becoming a Future-Ready Company," McKinsey & Company, January 11, 2021, https://www.mckinsey.com/business-functions/people-and-organizational-performance/our-insights/organizing-for-the-future-nine-keys-to-becoming-a-future-ready-company.

any evident rhyme or reason, nor did there seem to be any awareness on his part of the difference between coaching that was effective for the whole team and coaching that would be more effective one-on-one.

What I noticed in Marcus's behavior, though, was something that hadn't come through in the feedback I'd heard from his employees: when he was in one of his overly intense feedback moments, Marcus's body language and energy were totally focused on the person who was receiving the feedback. He seemed completely committed to their growth and understanding. By all appearances, he was truly in flow, deeply in a service mindset, and placed a high priority on his employees having the tools they needed to level up.

This tracked with what Eric had said about his own rapid personal and professional growth; Marcus was clearly an effective coach. And his team members deeply valued the growth they experienced working with him.

The change to be made was simple: Marcus needed to upgrade to platinum.

I booked a call with Marcus to give him the rundown on what I'd experienced observing his team. He enthusiastically accepted—a good sign. From everything I was seeing, Marcus's intentions were in exactly the right place.

After running through my initial feedback on the team with him—feedback he absorbed like a sponge, eagerly asking questions to make sure he understood every nugget of information—I asked him a simple question.

"How do your team members prefer to receive feedback on their performance?"

Marcus nodded, excited, and started talking a mile a minute. "The most effective thing I've found is to get them out of their comfort zone right off the bat. We share feedback all together in a group so that everyone gets the benefit of the lessons. And it can be a little uncomfortable—but their growth accelerates so much faster through that discomfort. They come through the other side so much stronger."

I let him go on for a bit, while noting that he'd done exactly as I predicted. Instead of answering my question, he was giving me an in-depth explanation of how he *gave* feedback.

I pointed this out. "That's not quite what I asked," I said. "I saw how you give feedback, and I can see the amazing growth your coaching has created in your team. But what I asked is a little different. How do they prefer to receive feedback?"

Like Andy, Emily, and so many other leaders I've worked with, a light bulb went off in Marcus's eyes.

"I don't know," he said, his speedy, excited tone slowing down for the first time in our conversation. "I've never asked that."

We dove into what it would look like to understand how each team member preferred to receive feedback, focusing on the boost to effectiveness that treating them the way *they* want to be treated would create.

"What you're doing now is definitely effective," I told him. "But how much *more* effective could it be if each team member felt like they knew exactly what to expect from you—because *you* know exactly how they'll receive your coaching best?"

Marcus and I didn't meet for another month, and on our next call, he was less enthusiastic.

"It's been a rough month," he admitted. "That one question—asking them how they want to receive feedback—it's kind of…blown the lid off. I had *no* idea the level to which *not* knowing how they wanted to be treated—and bulldozing ahead with putting them on the spot—was affecting their sense of trust and safety."

Good leaders take it hard when they realize they've been inadvertently causing harm. Like Lauren experienced, Marcus's realization that he'd unwittingly created an environment of distrust and fear hit him like a punch to the gut.

Platinum Leadership isn't *all* positive, all the time. Sometimes it's hard. Sometimes, as a leader, the biggest change and growth begins with you.

I coached Marcus to stick to the foundational actions that would build trust with his team. He committed to the practice with his usual enthusiasm, even though it meant an overhaul of his behavior. Instead of pushing his team members outside their comfort zone, he was, for the first time, the one on shaky, unpredictable ground. He got a firsthand sense of how a lack of psychological safety deeply affects every moment of one's day—and how building trust takes intention, focused action, and time.

Time being the operative word. As I mentioned, it took six months for Marcus to notice that his team was slowly coming alive in their newly safe environment.

"It's been a long winter," he told me in one of our sessions. "I feel like I've been waiting for spring to come for years. But I'm starting to see the sprouts emerging from the ground. The team feels like it has a new energy. I was so focused on growth before that I didn't think about trust. But growth without trust will eventually hit a ceiling."

"And do you feel that they trust you now?" I asked.

He paused, thinking, then responded, "It's growing. It's not all the way there, but it's growing. If I can keep sticking to what you've been telling me throughout this whole process—it begins with me—I know I can make the trust strong. I know I can sustain it."

"I know you can, too," I told him. "And yes—it does begin with you. But *it continues with them.* They're the ones that keep it going and make it grow. You may light the spark, but they're the ones who make the fireworks happen."

YOU GET SOLID: SELF-EVALUATION

1. Do you trust your leaders? Why or why not?

2. How does your sense of trust affect your day-to-day work?

3. Do you trust your team? What's one behavior they could exhibit that would make you feel more psychologically safe as their leader?

4. Do you know what safety feels like for each member of your team?

THEY GET SOLID: NEXT STEPS

1. Notice the questions: how often do the members of your team ask questions in group meetings? For those who rarely speak up, sit with each to determine what safety means to them.

2. Create an anonymous feedback line where team members can leave ideas, questions, and concerns they don't feel courageous enough to bring up. Be sure to individually respond to each, whether in word or action.

3. Schedule a team roundtable to discuss and define together the pillars of a judgment-free zone, then define a set of Team Commitments for creating it together. Don't forget to build in accountability measures; how will these commitments be upheld?

4. Conduct a "spot eval" with the team: create a table with each of the five team qualities defined by Project Aristotle, then ask each team member to rate the team on each quality from 1 to 5. Discuss the results as a team, and brainstorm ways to bring each number up.

7

GROW

In a time when over 3.5 million Americans are quitting their jobs each month, a staggering 94 percent of employees reported that they would stay at their company longer if the company invested time and resources in their professional growth.[81]

"I'm seriously considering faking my own death and fleeing to Argentina."

Cathy, my client of over a year and the COO of a large branding agency, kept her expression perfectly serious through the grainy video of her webcam.

"Okay," I said, laughing. "I'll bite. What's got you spooked this time?"

It wasn't the first time Cathy had dramatically announced her intention to disappear into the wind. One of my most naturally pessimistic clients, Cathy often struggled with seeing the opportunity in challenge. And now,

---

81 Abigail Johnson Hess, "LinkedIn: 94% of Employees Say They Would Stay at a Company Longer for This Reason—and It's Not a Raise," CNBC.com, February 27, 2019, https://www.cnbc.com/2019/02/27/94percent-of-employees-would-stay-at-a-company-for-this-one-reason.html.

she was facing the biggest challenge of her career. She had been tapped to speak to the *entire company* across two continents—over 6,000 employees—in a keynote kicking off their annual conference.

Cathy was a wreck.

"I'm usually the one *planning* the conference," she said, her voice ragged with anxiety. "That's what I do. I plan! I'm a planner. I execute. I make things happen. I get things done. I'm not the one in the spotlight—I'll *melt* in the spotlight."

I asked her why she thought the CEO had asked her to give the keynote.

"Beats me!"

Secretly, I already knew the answer. Cathy's CEO, Ian, had filled me in on his plan a week before he took Cathy aside and casually but firmly asked her to prepare to deliver the speech in six months' time. I had been waiting patiently for Cathy's panicked meeting request ever since. It had taken her all of a day to fulfill my expectations.

One of Cathy's biggest fears, and something we'd only barely touched on in our coaching work together, was public speaking. As she had described it to me once, "The worst thing anyone could ever do to me is put me onstage. I don't do karaoke. I don't give toasts at weddings. I don't even speak in front of small groups of friends. Me and the microphone are *not* friends."

That day on our call, I was better prepared to guide Cathy through the emotional freakout crashing down around her than she probably expected.

"Okay, so first of all—Cathy, you're going to give this keynote. And you're going to be *amazing.*"

Cathy's mouth dropped open. "Jackie!" she spluttered. "You're supposed to be on my side!"

"I am," I said. "I promise. We're going to do this together."

She frowned, speechless.

I schooled my expression into the most affable, confident, Jack-Dawson-from-*Titanic* grin I could muster. "Do you trust me?"

Begrudgingly, Cathy nodded. "I trust you." She continued, half joking, "I may not *like* you very much right now, but I trust you," with a bite to her tone that told me she was *way* out of her comfort zone.

"Then let's do this."

I was so well-prepared for that call, and for the following six months of coaching Cathy toward the biggest night of her career, because seven years earlier, I had been *exactly* where she was. I didn't have the same generalized fear of public speaking, but when I was invited for the first time to speak to an audience of thousands, rather than dozens, I had the same initial reaction of fear—and I had a long journey of stretching my skills and confidence to prepare me for that stage.

If I could stretch that far, I knew Cathy could. Getting stretchy was where we needed to start.

THE SAFETY TO STRETCH

Each year, my family makes multiple visits to Sun Valley, Idaho. We always choose to drive from our home in Colorado—a thirteen-hour drive (we choose to drive so we can bring our dog, a Newfie named Hailey, aka Big Nazty). When they were younger and not as deeply immersed in YouTube, my two sons played a game on these long road trips. They'd pick a word, any word—*fork, plane, candle*—and say it over and over until the word completely lost its meaning for all of us.

Believe me, hearing two stir-crazy elementary aged boys chant, *"Candle! Candle! Candle! Candle!"* on repeat for fifteen minutes on end (or until, clinging to sanity, I put a firm end to it) is a quick road to questioning your life choices.

The boys' word game, and my resulting headache, is what often comes to mind for me when I hear the phrase "get out of your comfort zone." This saying is so ubiquitous in the workplace that it's practically lost all meaning.

And yet when the topic of employee growth comes up in conversation, it's often the first tip given. There's a pervasive idea that the only way a person can truly level up their performance is if they spend some time flailing in the deep end of the pool before finally, out of sheer survival instinct, getting the hang of treading water in their new circumstance.

Recall Marcus's reasoning for his rapid-fire, intense public feedback sessions: *I get them out of their comfort zone right off the bat. They come through the other side so much stronger.*

Stronger, maybe—but also terrified, and dreading the next grenade lobbed their way.

Growth happens best in a psychologically safe environment. So why do so many leaders work against psychological safety by pushing their employees into an uncomfortable and fearful state in the name of growth?

The process of growth and learning definitely involves nudging yourself toward the edge of your comfort zone, but it doesn't require entering a fear state. In fact, when we're in a fear state, it's *harder* to learn and grow. In that state, our brains are flooded with stress hormones like cortisol and adrenaline. The amygdala, the part of the brain that governs emotions, becomes hypersensitive to threats, ready at any moment to tell the hypothalamus to activate a fight-or-flight reaction. Your brain's watchman is on high alert, seeing every shadow in every direction as an army of bears that threatens your very existence.

Meanwhile, the connection between your amygdala and your prefrontal cortex—the link between emotion and reason—begins to break down. The prefrontal cortex comes up with a rational, logical response: *those aren't bears, they're just shadows.* But it isn't heard over the din of your amygdala screaming, *Bear! Bear! Bear! Bear!* with the same unrelenting chant as two boys in the back of an SUV, on hour ten of the drive from Denver to Sun Valley.

Without the ability to rationally process input, the brain's capacity to learn from that input is compromised. Any lessons that could inspire growth get lost in the fray.

Growth doesn't need to mean getting completely *out* of your comfort zone. It's possible to have both—the strengthening effect of bumping up against discomfort and coming through it, and the safety of a calm, rational mind that can soak up new information and learn the lessons it offers.

The trick is to push yourself into discomfort while staying in the optimistic part of your brain where you can still see possibilities, overcome challenges, and make progress. That's the sweet spot.

This is what I call *getting stretchy*, and it's where you and your team can explore unrestrained, exponential growth.

Have you ever been lost in a shopping mall? Picture one of those giant lit-up maps you study in an effort to figure out how the heck you could have traversed the mall four times and still not found the Nordstrom. You always zoom in first on the all-caps label with the big red dot: YOU ARE HERE. Then you carefully set landmarks on the journey to your destination: *Okay, straight ahead until the Spencer's Gifts...then hang a left... then another left at Brookstone's...then take the escalator next to Auntie Annie's and it should be right there.*

This is how I like to think of getting stretchy. First, you find your current place of comfort (YOU ARE HERE), and then map the place outside that zone that you want to reach (Nordstrom). Once you have this destination in mind, you create small, intentional, and deliberate steps to get there. By breaking your path into bite-sized (read: less panic-inducing) pieces, you're able to conquer your fears without having to scare the wits out of yourself in the process.

When we stretch ourselves like this, we give ourselves time to build the elasticity we need to adjust to each new micro-risk along the path. And we do this minus the code-red alarms that go off in our brains when we jump into the abyss outside our comfort zone and set our nervous system on fire.

Instead of terrifying, deep water where we have to sink or swim, we end up right where we want to go, and reestablish a new normal. We grow happily, comfortably, and most importantly, faster than we would have through a fog of fear.

Getting stretchy doesn't mean you won't be nervous about the challenge in front of you, but it does mean you'll be mindful about preparing yourself for what's ahead—and that's when the learning occurs.

The essence of getting stretchy is putting in the work and practice that allows you to reach a place where you can say to yourself: *I'm ready for this. I've worked my way up to this moment in a deliberate way, and this is now within my band of comfort.*

You might be at the furthest boundary of your comfort zone, your heart might still be beating faster, you might have butterflies in your stomach, but you're not in fight-or-flight. You're not hypersensitive and seeing bears all around you. Instead, you're rational, grounded, and receptive to experience. You're ready to learn and evolve.

STRESS KILLS—TEAMS, PRODUCTIVITY, AND GROWTH

As a leader, reducing stress in your team is a top priority.

That sounds like one of those "duh!" moments I talked about in the Introduction—but truly, systemic stress is so catastrophic to organizations, it's a wonder the idea of "getting out of your comfort zone" ever took hold at all.

First of all, let's define stress. When people are subjected to negative emotions, fear states, high pressure, confusion, and anger, it creates a physical storm of stress hormones inside the body. Cortisol and adrenaline, which are supposed to spike when a threat arises—to get you running away from the bear—and otherwise stay low, are cranked up to a constant simmer, bringing with them a whole host of ailments. Dozens of health markers, from quality sleep to blood pressure to cognitive ability, plummet when we're in a state of stress.

Stress doesn't make us stronger. It makes us unhappy, unhealthy, and desperate for relief.

What's more, it's *expensive.*

The American Psychological Association estimates that more than $500 billion is siphoned off from the US economy annually because of workplace stress. On top of that, 550 million workdays are lost each year due to stress on the job (I triple checked this stat—you read that number right).[82] Sixty percent to 80 percent of workplace accidents are attributed to stress,[83] and it's estimated that more than 80 percent of doctor visits have stress as a central factor.[84] Workplace stress has been linked to health problems ranging from metabolic syndrome to cardiovascular disease—and, ultimately, mortality.

Stress is just as contagious as emotion. Secondhand stress is *very* real. A separate group of researchers found that 26 percent of people showed elevated levels of cortisol just by *observing* someone who was stressed.[85]

---

82 Gustavo Razzetti, "Burnout: The Reason Your Team Is Not Innovating," *Forbes*, February 6, 2020, https://www.forbes.com/sites/forbescoachescouncil/2020/02/06/burnout-the-reason-your-team-is-not-innovating/?sh=3d19adf13763.

83 Seppälä and Cameron, "Proof That Positive Work Cultures."

84 Beth Israel Deaconess Medical Center, "Stress Management Counseling in the Primary Care Setting Is Rare," ScienceDaily, November 19, 2012, https://www.sciencedaily.com/releases/2012/11/121119163258.htm.

85 Shawn Achor and Michelle Gielan, "Make Yourself Immune to Secondhand Stress," *Harvard Business Review*, September 2, 2015, https://hbr.org/2015/09/make-yourself-immune-to-second-hand-stress#:~:text=Observing%20someone%20who%20is%20stressed,observing%20some-one%20who%20was%20stressed.

As a leader practicing the Platinum Rule, you've already created an environment of psychological safety. Your team members exist in a judgment-free zone where they feel heard, seen, and courageously honest. With this sense of safety comes a cascade of oxytocin, the bonding chemical we discussed earlier. Oxytocin is a direct counteragent to cortisol. It reduces anxiety, lowers blood pressure, encourages positive social connection, and promotes feelings of trust and well-being.

Staying within the boundaries of psychological safety is imperative for your team to truly realize its growth potential. The practice of getting stretchy begins from the safety place and slowly, gradually, moves the goalposts outward. You want someone to bump up against the edge of their comfort zone, but never hurl past it—to expand their comfort zone, not abandon it. The continued feeling of safety allows people to open themselves to taking risks, play beyond their boundaries, and ultimately, level up their baseline of skill, ability, and motivation.

Stress in Numbers

- A recent Northwestern National Life survey showed that 40 percent of workers rated their jobs as "extremely stressful."[86]

- Studies strongly associate workplace stress with obesity, high cholesterol, high blood pressure, and even heart attack and stroke.[87]

---

86 "Workplace Stress: A Silent Killer of Employee Health and Productivity," *Corporate Wellness Magazine*, https://www.corporatewellnessmagazine.com/article/workplace-stress-silent-killer-employee-health-productivity.

87 Ibid.

- Workers who report high workplace stress are more likely to smoke, abuse alcohol and drugs, and eat an unhealthy diet.[88]

- The WHO recently found that in one year, workplace stress accounted for $190 billion in healthcare spending in the United States, cost businesses $1 trillion in lost productivity, and led to 120,000 deaths.[89]

STRETCH IN ACTION

Creating a Stretchy practice involves doing something many people avoid: not just identifying and calling out, but looking *directly* at their deepest fear.

As a leader, you can help your team members get stretchy with the following practice.

Action #1: Reframe the Fear

One of my good friends is a lifelong spotlight-lover. As a kid, she did community theater; in high school, she starred in each year's musical;

---

88   Ibid.

89   Aleksandar Dimovski, "19 Workplace Stress Statistics That Will Make You Wonder," GoRe-motely.net, November 8, 2021, https://goremotely.net/blog/workplace-stress-statistics/.

in college, she had a scholarship in Speech and Debate, and toured the country behind a series of podiums, regularly speaking before audiences of 1,000-plus.

I once asked her if she ever got stage fright. "Sort of," she responded.

She shared a stage trick with me she'd learned early on. "The physical sensations of fear and excitement are exactly alike," she told me. "So whenever I feel nerves, I tell myself I'm just excited to go out there and crush it. My body doesn't know the difference, and my brain lets go of its fear-based thinking."

Getting stretchy begins with a reframe of your fear. When you think of your physical reaction to a new, stretchy challenge—heart pounding, sweaty palms, trembling—as excitement rather than nervousness, you've already reframed the direction of your action toward a positive outcome rather than a fear state.

Action #2: Comfortably Uncomfortable

No need to wait for Getting Stretchy to feel "normal"—it's always going to be a little bit uncomfortable, and that's by design.

As such, acknowledging right away that your stretchy space is going to have a few spikes and slippery spots is crucial. Rose-colored glasses simply mask red flags. Go into getting stretchy with the full acceptance of the discomfort inherent in the experience.

But also, give yourself forward momentum by tacking "yet" onto the end of each new thing you're learning how to do. Carol Dweck, a Stanford

University professor of Psychology and author of *Mindset*, calls this "the power of *yet*."

I can't command a room of 6,000 people...yet.

I can't write a speech, let alone get through it without stumbling...yet.

By adding the word "yet," these limiting statements—which lead to limiting beliefs—lose their limits. What was a *can't* becomes a future *can*.

Create the mindspace that your stretched-out comfort zone is a whole new shape and size to live into. You'll get stretchy through a vision of your future that includes your destination, rather than where you're stuck right now.

Action #3: Share Your Own Stretch

As the leader, you can create safety for your team to get stretchy by sharing the areas where you yourself are currently stretching—and creating authentic connection around shared discomfort.

Let's reflect back to our previous discussion on sharing your mistakes. Humanizing yourself for the people you lead is a huge trust-builder, and asking team members to stretch their comfort zone is much more enthusiastically met when they can see you stretching yours as well.

I once worked with a client for whom the very act of sharing that she needed to stretch with her team *was* getting stretchy. She was terrified that if she showed her team that she didn't have all the answers, wasn't perfect at everything, and needed to grow in certain areas, they'd stop trusting her. The idea of being honest and open about her areas of growth was a huge stretch.

Your team doesn't expect you to know and be good at everything. If you did, you'd be a robot. Show them your stretchy side, and they'll feel permission to show theirs.

Action #4: Shared Stretching

You know how going to the gym is always easier when you've got a friend sweating alongside you? There's something about shared discomfort that makes it easier to push through.

The same goes for getting stretchy. Pull your team together and define a stretch goal that gets everyone bumping up against the boundaries of their comfort zone—maybe completing a project within a faster timeframe, or shooting for a big-vision goal that's going to demand growth from everyone in order to achieve. Create a plan together to accomplish this goal.

Finally, have everyone choose an accountability partner on the team to hold them to their growth. That sense of shared discomfort, and holding each other to the goals they set, creates a deeper bond of camaraderie and trust between teammates.

Key Concept: Practical Optimism

Optimism is one of the most commonly misunderstood concepts out there. I see it all the time in my coaching. People mistake *optimism* for "all rainbows and butterflies, all the time," dismissing actual problems in favor of a falsely positive attitude.

Avoidance of reality isn't what we're going for with practical optimism. It's not about pretending bad things aren't bad, or that nothing ever goes wrong.

Rather, practical optimism looks toward the future. Faced with a setback, the optimist asks themselves: *What do I want to do about it? What are my choices? What possibilities are present?* They also seek out social support and face the setback head-on. The optimist operates with an innate belief that together, we can get through anything.

A quote I love that I feel perfectly describes the *practice* of optimism, and its opposite, comes from Winston Churchill: "A pessimist sees the difficulty in every opportunity; an optimist sees the opportunity in every difficulty."

Optimism is rooted in the choice you make when faced with a setback: seeing the bear, or seeing a harmless shadow that can be fixed with the right amount of light.

Optimism is correlated with a whole host of positive physical and emotional outcomes. People who practice optimism tend to have better mental and physical health—they literally don't get sick as often, and they heal faster. In one study of patients who had undergone heart surgery, those patients with an optimistic outlook were half as likely to require rehospitalization after six months as patients who were more pessimistic.[90] The results are the same at work; a workplace study of 11,308 employees found that employees who showed high optimism were 103 percent more inspired to do their best work.[91]

When a leader approaches the problem with confidence in a positive outcome, you can almost feel the stress and anxiety releasing from the group. Look, it's going to be okay. We can do this.

STRETCHY, NOT SCARY

Cathy's panic over the prospect of giving her company's keynote was a reaction I recognized. It was the same reaction I'd had when I was invited to give my first big talk on leadership.

The convention I was invited to speak at was being held at the Denver Performing Arts Center, a venue that seats 2,000. At that point in my career, the largest group I'd spoken in front of was a series of workshops for an audience of 100.

---

90 "Optimism and Your Health," Harvard Health Publishing, May 1, 2008, https://www.health.harvard.edu/heart-health/optimism-and-your-health.

91 Mark Murphy, "Optimistic Employees Are 103% More Inspired to Give Their Best Effort at Work, New Data Reveals," *Forbes*, February 26, 2020, https://www.forbes.com/sites/markmurphy/2020/02/26/optimistic-employees-are-103-more-inspired-to-give-their-best-effort-at-work-new-data-reveals/?sh=480f0a607afc.

Needless to say, I was terrified. Visions of a doctored passport and the rolling hills of South America *definitely* flashed through my mind.

I was so terrified, in fact, that it took me a full two days to tell anyone that I'd been asked to speak. I didn't call back the convention planner. I left the email confirming my attendance in my inbox, rereading it and marking it unread again over and over.

Essentially, I pretended like nothing had happened. This usually only works if you have a partner less intuitive than mine. Two days after the invitation, Rob stopped me from obsessively rewashing a batch of clean dishes that had just come out of the dishwasher.

"What is going on with you?" he demanded. "You're wound tighter than an antique clock."

I confessed about the invitation to speak at the conference. He looked at me with shock, obviously baffled.

"Why did you wait so long to tell me?"

"Because I didn't want it to be real!" I said, already feeling the muscles in my arms begin to tremble just thinking about the speech. "I know I have to do it. I know it'll be great for my career. But I'm scared to death!"

Rob didn't need to say anything. Just by speaking the fear out loud, I knew what my next move was.

I needed to stretch to meet the speech. That stage was my destination, and I had my GPS coordinates dialed in. Progress forward was up to me.

The first thing I did when I accepted the invitation to speak (besides screaming into a pillow after clicking "send" on the confirmation email) was ask the event organizers for a list of the other confirmed speakers. Within an hour, I had a list of potential coaches at my fingertips.

I reached out to a Hall of Fame speaker named Molly, who was internationally known in the industry and had given enough talks that her fee could buy her a new car after each appearance.

After explaining my situation, and making the extent of my discomfort clear without actually saying the words "I'm in a panic spiral," I simply asked for the help I needed. *Could I pay you for coaching?*

Molly agreed, sending back a coaching agreement that same day. Her only demand: that she do it for free. Not only that, but she invited me to her house for coaching sessions, and always met me at the front door with a cup of hot tea. Talk about creating a safe environment!

Over the next four months leading up to the speech, I devoted myself to preparation. After all, what's a better fear-killer than being prepared? The Boy Scouts could have learned a thing or two from my speech prep.

Step by step, I pushed up against my comfort zone. I addressed each of my fears one by one and created a new normal with each step I advanced forward.

Meanwhile, I remained realistic about the fact that my heart would likely be racing as I took the stage. (I was getting stretchy, not delusional— there was no scenario in which nerves would be completely eradicated.)

But I also knew that I had given myself the time and space to become jazzed up about the challenge, excited about my growth. I was terrified, sure, but I wouldn't be scared into speechlessness.

When the day arrived, I nervously shuffled my speech notecards over and over as Rob drove me to the venue. I'd created the notecards as a little crutch to prop me up—just in case I got so nervous that all of my other cues didn't work. All of the mentors I'd spoken to in the past four months had shared that they used cards the first few times they spoke in front of large audiences, too.

In the end, I didn't need them. The speech went fantastic; I sailed through it without a hitch, and the cards stayed untouched on the podium. I got terrific feedback and was ultimately invited to speak at several other conferences around the country as a result of that starting point. It was a great experience, and exactly the growth opportunity I had known it could be even as I was avoiding calling the event organizer back.

Had I plunged immediately past my comfort zone, I would have been stuck in a fear state, unable to learn what I needed to feel confident on that stage. (I also probably would have passed out the moment I crossed the convention center threshold.)

As it was, the preparation I'd been able to do while finding and staying within my space of safety—and then stretching the edges of my tolerance for several months to encompass more and more distance toward my goal—was key to my success. Standing on that stage, listening to my voice echo out across the crowded convention center, I felt proud, accomplished, and confident. *I can do this, now and anytime I want in the future.* It's a feeling that hasn't left me in years since.

I stretched, I grew, and I didn't shrink back down to my original comfort zone. Getting stretchy changes the boundaries of that zone to encompass more and more with each new stretch.

BUSINESS BREAKTHROUGHS

We've already covered the staggering cost to businesses created by employee turnover. Growth and professional development play a key role in employee retention; employees who report a lack of investment in their development are three times more likely to be looking for a new job.[92] Meanwhile, an incredible 94 percent of employees say they'd stay in their job longer if their company invested in their professional growth![93] Stretchy employees are happy employees who return the investment made in them back to the business tenfold. Those who stretch are also more practiced in taking risks—and risks lead to innovation, an integral component of any company's success.

BIG NIGHT

With my experience getting stretchy in the *exact* same scenario, I knew the particular challenges, roadblocks, and pitfalls that awaited Cathy.

---

92 Kate Heinz, "42 Shocking Company Culture Statistics You Need to Know," Builtin.com, October 2, 2019, https://builtin.com/company-culture/company-culture-statistics.

93 Hess, "LinkedIn: 94% of Employees Say They Would Stay."

I also knew the joy of her destination. I was determined to help her get there.

Over the course of the six months before the keynote, Cathy *stretched*. We started putting her on panels at different conferences where she could be on stage with other experts and take questions from the audience—smaller scale, to be sure, but a low-stakes way to help her get comfortable in the spotlight.

Then she started giving one-off presentations to team members on different topics, which helped her feel more comfortable when the spotlight was solely on her.

Next up, we started recording her speeches on camera, so she could see how she presented herself and find ways to hone her delivery.

When the big day arrived six months later, she was prepared.

"I can't believe it," she told me during our session the day before the keynote. "In fact, I almost *don't* believe it. I feel nervous, but I also feel… confident. I feel like this is a challenge I'll rise to."

She laughed out loud. "Six months ago, can you even imagine me saying that? I wanted to run away to Argentina!"

On the speaking stage the next day, Cathy knew her material, felt comfortable in the setting, and had practiced enough that she could hold the audience's attention with confidence and skill. The nerves didn't go away, but I could tell she'd put a lot of work into reframing her emotions.

"Every time my hands shook, I told myself it was with excitement," she said later, recounting what had been an incredibly successful keynote speech. "Every time I swallowed involuntarily, I just used it as a natural pause in my speaking cadence to make the speech flow better. Each challenge, I rewrote as an opportunity."

"You know what this means," I told her.

"What?"

"Ian wants you to give the keynote next year, too. That's a job well d—"

"I'll stop you right there," Cathy interrupted me. "I may have stretched my comfort zone, but I'm not embarking on a career change here. One and done is enough for me! I did it, I grew, and now I'm ready to *never meet a microphone again.*"

YOU GET SOLID: SELF-EVALUATION

1. Notice where you might improve as a leader looking back at feedback from one-on-ones and 360s. Create an action plan, micro-action-steps to move in that direction—without stretching so much that you shut down or quit.

2. How will this stretch goal help you?

3. How will it help your team?

4. Create a timeline and share your stretch journey with an accountability partner.

THEY GET SOLID: NEXT STEPS

1. Have each member of the team create a stretch goal and a plan for getting there, with a clear deadline.

2. Set up accountability partners and track progress publicly, with each stop on the stretch journey mapped out and celebrated.

3. Finally, work together to define a stretch goal for the whole team. Give each team member a role in tracking progress and holding the team accountable.

8

WIN

In a *Harvard Business Review* study of nearly 12,000 daily
employee diary entries, the most common event triggering a
"best day" was *any progress* in the work by the person or team.[94]

"I never thought I'd say this, but the problem is that he's *too* good."

I was speaking with Eleanor, the VP of Development of a booming wearable tech company. Eleanor had an odd problem on her hands. Her star player, Colin, an energetic forty-year-old who led the largest development team, had the distinction of leading *the* "cool kid" team at the company, that everyone wanted to be on—and yet the motivation and morale on the team was troublingly low.

And when I say low, I mean *low*. If the team itself could wear one of the company's devices, it would constantly be beeping with those mildly condescending motivational pushes that make you sigh and begrudgingly get up to stretch your legs. *You've been sitting still for hours! It's time to move.* (I wanted to track my steps, not get scolded by the cloud…sheesh!)

---

94 Teresa M. Amabile and Steven J. Kramer, "The Power of Small Wins," *Harvard Business Review*, May 2011, https://hbr.org/2011/05/the-power-of-small-wins.

Colin was, to put it mildly, an absolute dynamo. He was genius-level smart, an idea factory, and his work was light years beyond anyone else's, in his division or anywhere else in the company. He was easygoing, too—friendliness and likability weren't the problem.

The problem was that he was leaving everyone on his team behind.

These weren't people who were accustomed to being left behind. The best and brightest got chosen to work on Colin's team. They developed the coolest new products, they had a fat budget, and their launches were huge events, with media and tech bloggers descending like locusts to check out the newest wearables. *Everyone* wanted to be on Colin's team. It was the winning team, and he was the captain.

And yet somehow, no one on his team *felt* like a winner. In fact, they felt like losers.

None of them were anything less than a rockstar themselves. If you're a rockstar, you're in the top 1 percent of your craft; you're famous, you have some gold records, maybe a couple of hits on the Billboard Top 20. People stop you on the street and ask for a picture. You're a big deal.

But then Taylor Swift roars into town on a multi-platinum arena tour, and suddenly you're small potatoes. After all, there are rockstars, and then there are *superstars*.

Colin was a superstar. No one on his team could compare.

"The work is great. That team reliably churns out our biggest-selling new products, and they're always innovating in ways the industry can't predict," Eleanor told me. "But when you talk to the people on the team individually, it's like they think they're barely making the grade. They're getting A-pluses on every test, but they're walking around like they're failing out of school."

The people on the team had no sense of their wins for two big reasons. One was just the nature of the beast: the product development timeline from idea to launch was, at the shortest, two years. This meant that the team developing a new product had a long two-year runway of antici-pation before they saw the results. In a company as big and scaling as quickly as theirs, team members often quickly got promoted or rotated to other teams, so by the time a product hit the market, the original team who had developed it was no longer around to celebrate its success.

This problem, the long runway to the win, wasn't helped by Colin's lead-ership. He was so fast, so smart, and so ahead of the game that the rest of his team never even got a look at the goal line—he had blown past it before they even set foot on the field. They were trailing in his wake, feeling like they were constantly too slow and clumsy.

"I ran into Jennifer, one of our junior designers, the other day in the eleva-tor—this is a young woman we just hired out of MIT who's a phenom-enal talent. She made a comment that basically told me she feels like an idiot all the time." Eleanor sighed and shook her head. "It's ridiculous. And it's a crazy problem, because how do you tell a superstar to…shine less brightly? I don't know what to do. But something needs to change, because morale is in the dumps, and it's spreading with every water-cooler conversation." (That pesky emotional contagion again!)

I knew I was going to need to get in there with Colin's team to assess the situation, but I also knew immediately that the solution wasn't what Eleanor was thinking. No *way* did she want Colin shining less brightly. Fixing morale didn't have to mean pulling Colin back from his best work.

What needed to happen was a reframe of what "best work" meant— centered around all the other team members, not just Colin.

The team needed to see and recognize their *own* wins.

WHY SMALL WINS MATTER

Big goals are great, and the sweet victory of finally achieving them after years of hard work is definitely cause for massive celebration. Good things come to those who wait, and the buildup of energy and anticipation in waiting for a long-sought-after win does indeed feel amazing.

But how do you keep motivation, morale, and excitement high through-out the entire waiting period? How do you keep the energy up today, when the goal line is years in the future?

The key is smaller incremental celebrations as you move toward the goal—defining wins as not just the big thing that happens at the end, but as everyday successes and positive moments that create the sensation of forward progress. Because It's *progress*, no matter how small, that has the biggest psychological impact on motivation.

This is one of the reasons people love wearable tech like the kind made by Colin's team of rockstars. A step counter on your wrist buzzes to let you know you're "almost there"—even if you're only at the halfway point. If your steps are clicking up, your total keeps rising, if there's evidence *you have in fact gotten off the couch*, the momentary celebration is a way to ensure you keep at it.

Wins in Numbers

- Research shows the more a team celebrates their success together, the better their chances are of winning. A 2010 study of basketball teams found that teams who physically celebrated most with congratulatory taps, fist bumps, hugs, pats, and high-fives also cooperated more, and won the most games.[95]

- In a HBR study that compared research participants' best and worst days (based on their overall mood, specific emotions, and motivation levels), researchers found that the most common event triggering a "best day" was any progress in the work by the individual or the team.[96]

When you achieve something, your brain releases dopamine, a "feel good" neurotransmitter. It does this whether the trigger is big or small, and is outcome-agnostic—meaning, it doesn't actually matter if the outcome is *good* for you. Your brain doesn't care about the outcome; it releases dopamine either way. The same mechanism that makes it feel good to get a shoutout for your awesome presentation deck at the all-hands meeting— or a flurry of likes on that Instagram you posted of your dog wearing

---

95 Stephanie Pappas, "Touchy-Feely NBA Teams More Likely to Win," NBCNews.com, November 12, 2010, https://www.nbcnews.com/health/health-news/touchy-feely-nba-teams-more-likely-win-flna1c9471843.

96 Amabile and Kramer, "The Power of Small Wins."

sunglasses—also gives you a pleasure boost when you get that buzz on your wrist. Or, sometimes to our detriment, that next donut or glass of wine.

These dopamine "hits" are a big part of our internal reward system. This system causes us to seek out more of whatever gave us the feeling of pleasure.

This is why many people first hear about dopamine in the context of addiction. But the dopamine hits themselves are not inherently *good* or *bad*. They're activated in goal-directed behavior that's good for you—completing a task at work—and bad for you—downing too many vodka shots at a best friend's wedding.

Progress is dopamine working *for* you. Wins make you want more wins. And just as wonderful, your brain starts to anticipate the pleasure that wins elicit. You naturally keep moving in the direction of the win with each micro-choice you make moment to moment.

It's fascinating brain science, but in a way, it's simple, too. The feedback loop goes like this:

1. You receive great feedback or hit a milestone at work.

2. Dopamine is activated; you feel pleasure.

3. You want to do it again.

You optimize this brain behavior by creating initial feelings of success, then providing frequent opportunities to achieve small wins *on the way to larger and more challenging goals*. As a leader, you create the spark by helping your team find wins. Then you repeat, continuing to throw on kindling until it becomes a fire.

Some scientists say dopamine is what makes us human. While our brains are very similar to chimpanzees', the gene responsible for producing dopamine is turned on in humans, but not apes, according to a 2017 study in *Science*.[97]

Progress is important to us not just as leaders, but as a species. It's part of what makes us—all of us—able to accomplish amazing things…and feel awesome doing it.

HOW TO FIND WINS—EVEN IN HARD TIMES

We've established you need to feel wins to stay engaged. It's biological. And sometimes, finding wins is easy—you gained a big client, you got it done under budget and under time. Other times it's…not so easy.

Such is life.

So what happens when the wins are hard to find? In stressful times, when there's a high workload or timing for a big project is tight or you're facing losing an important client—or, I don't know, there's a global pandemic (I know, sounds crazy, but it happens!)—wins are scarce.

Sometimes, finding wins is like those games on the back of a kids' menu. Your child is supposed to find the six candy canes in a super busy picture. They ask for help and you, a grown adult, search and search and just can't find that last candy cane. You swear it's not there.

---

97 André M. M. Sousa et al., "Molecular and Cellular Reorganization of Neural Circuits in the Human Lineage," *Science* 358 no. 6366 (2017): 1027–1032, https://www.science.org/doi/full/10.1126/science.aan3456.

That's come up a lot, lately, for my clients.

We can't find a win because we don't have any.

We're in a high-stress time.

We're losing our accounts.

The board's really scrutinizing us.

All you can see is the negative, because you're conditioned to see it more quickly and clearly than the positive—when times are rough, the bear pops out from behind every corner and every curtain.

During the pandemic, one of my clients, an advertising agency, was struggling. Most of their clients had paused operations, and had put nonessential expenses—like advertising—on hold.

My clients were taking call after call about canceling. Their clients didn't need to buy advertising for the simple, immutable reason that they were closed for business, with no idea when they'd reopen.

I worked with them to find the wins, and was met with a brick wall. *There are no wins. Everything is awful.*

So, instead I focused them on recalibrating their goals. After all, when you can't win the game, change it.

The questions I had them focus on became "What are our goals *right now*? What is a win *right now*?"

The answer was clear: make sure that when, if, circumstances changed, all their clients would come back.

Once this new goal was set, ideas started flowing. Within days, a series of return-to-work contracts were created and signed with as many current clients as possible. It wasn't the win they originally thought they needed, with the goalpost shifted, it was still a score.

When times get tough, creating new goals is essential. Your team needs to feel like they're heading toward something achievable they can celebrate. Their brains want to anticipate a win and feel that dopamine rush. Sometimes that can only happen if goals are adjusted.

How do you do this? First, recognize and acknowledge that things have shifted. As a leader, you don't have the luxury of denial. Ask yourself what is achievable and realistic in the current situation.

Once you create more long-term objectives, though, you're not finished. Remember, they need to be broken down into smaller, achievable hits, or wins, that your team can celebrate along the way.

WINNING THE PLATINUM MEDAL

Everyone has a different definition of a win, and your work as a leader involves consistently discovering what motivates your team members.

This is where Colin struggled. The way he conceived of a win was on a completely different scale from the rest of his team, because he was so far ahead in natural ability. Because he saw wins on *his* scale, he never recognized the wins his team was achieving on *their* scale.

As a leader practicing Platinum, your first step is finding out what qualifies as a win to your team.

I've found that people generally perceive a win as anything you can check off that represents progress toward a goal. It's moving forward, something that propels you toward those numbers to the right of neutral. And not only that—the *closer* the win appears, the more motivated you are to drive toward it. This is called the *goal gradient effect*, and has been studied by psychologists and behavioral scientists for decades; the closer you are to the finish line, the faster you run.

Showing wins visually goes a long way.

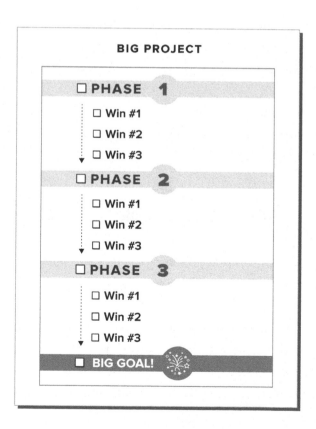

When there's a large, looming project, having a shared whiteboard, physical or virtual, is helpful. On the board, divide the project into sections, or mini-goals that must be hit along the way to accomplish the ultimate project goal.

As you complete small goals, check them off and celebrate in whatever way makes sense for your team. When you frame it that way, in measurable sections instead of *we still have 75 percent to go*, the feeling of unending stress is replaced with the feeling of success, of accomplishment.

Once, a few years back, I was working with a thirteen-person team working on a three-year conversion of many company systems. So, again, same as with Colin's product development team: *long* runway to success. As a result, a year and a half into the conversion, they had lost motivation. On top of that, the company had recently needed to make resource cuts, and the team had lost five key members. Workloads for everyone else rose dramatically. By the time I began working with them, they were working night and day with almost no time off. People weren't getting them what they needed. Things were behind.

The energy in the room I walked into wasn't just low—it was negative, defeated, *bad*.

"All right, guys," I said, clapping my hands. "We need to find some wins." I stood in front of a large whiteboard, marker in hand, poised to write down anything that was called out.

At first, I heard crickets. A room of defeated, skeptical faces stared back at me silently. Then, finally, a few comments began to spill out—but they were dire.

"There's nothing positive going on."

"It's so stressful."

"We're so overwhelmed."

"Everybody sucks." (Ouch.)

I tried a different approach. "Okay, let's start *really* small. Did anybody…I don't know, get through the week without a Zoom meeting crashing?" I asked.

A few nodded. "That's positive!" I said. "Let's put it on the board. What else?"

At first, it was quiet. As I said, these people were *burnt*. But then.

"Actually, my Zoom did crash, but Frank was on the call, and he was able to finish it for me."

"The team in Arizona finally got back to us after about a million follow-ups."

I could see them starting to realize that a win doesn't have to be a big, shiny thing—a win is *any* progress.

"They brought in lunch for us on Monday. That was fun and a nice surprise."

"Oh yeah, and then Lisa helped me with this thing, and I was able to leave early…"

Each win they named, no matter how small, I wrote on the whiteboard. Soon we had a whiteboard full of wins. Being able to see the wins visually shifted the energy of the room—people started to unfreeze a little. It was only the beginning of my work with them, and we still had a long way to go, but it was a positive start that made room for practical optimism going forward.

As a Platinum Leader, you know the way your team wants to be treated—and you know what individually motivates each of them. As such, you can craft and facilitate the specific wins that will fire up your team. Two actions can facilitate this.

Action #1: Ask

You have an idea what wins could look like for your team, but you need their input as well. Ask these questions:

"What does a win feel like to you?"

"As you look back on this project, what were some wins you experienced? What felt good? What gave you a sense of accomplishment?

You might be surprised by what you hear—because, remember, what feels good to someone else may not be what feels good to you. If you find yourself thinking, *Seriously? That would pump you up?* when a team member shares their answers, it might be time to go Platinum with them to make sure you're on the same page.

Action #2: Pay Attention

The second thing you need to do is to be on the lookout for progress. When you spot it, call it out.

I know this was a tough week, but despite that, I noticed that you ultimately were able to resolve this problem—it's been dragging on forever! That's a big win!

Just calling it out is a celebration. Sometimes, a person might not notice their win because it was natural or got buried in the negative. Like platinum, sometimes you need to go deep to mine the wins. And when you do point out a win someone missed, it'll probably make them feel *great*. They'll get a dopamine hit.

Once you spark a "wins" mindset, momentum builds. Soon, your whole team will be speaking the language of wins, propelling themselves and each other forward. I think of it like a tumbleweed—a pretty one, mind you, rolling along a field of sunflowers, gathering mass and energy as it moves toward its destination.

CELEBRATE, CELEBRATE, CELEBRATE

Because progress is the key to motivation, and motivation is essential to achieving goals, celebrating any form of progress isn't silly or indulgent. It's critical. But it can be hard to believe that.

I work with a funny, fierce CFO named Jane who had a bit of a hang-up about doling out praise to her team.

"It feels like overkill to praise them for achieving the basic results of their job," she told me. "If we're celebrating every little thing they do, what's to stop them from becoming complacent? I want them to strive to be *better*."

Fair. But there was a whole Gulf of Mexico between "celebrating every little thing they do" and what Jane was doing, which was, essentially, *never* celebrating *anything*.

Her team was afraid to come to her with questions; they didn't think they were doing a good job or meeting her standards or expectations. Their psychological safety was nil. As a result, their ability to get stretchy—her intention in the first place—was low, and motivation was down, not up.

Jane's leadership style isn't unusual. In a *Harvard Business Review* (HBR) study about the keys to motivating workers, very few managers ranked "progress" first. Things like clear goals, interpersonal support, and tangible incentives ranked higher.[98]

Another HBR survey of more than 12,000 employee daily diary entries proved the point. People were more creative and productive when their inner work lives were positive, rather than dominated by fear and pressure. And what contributed most to a positive inner work life? "Steps forward," write the researchers. *Wins.*[99]

The more frequently people experience a sense of progress, the more likely they are to be creatively productive in the long run. That's because inner work life drives performance; in turn, good performance, which depends on consistent progress, enhances inner work life. HBR calls this the "progress loop."[100]

An easy real-world example? Football.

---

98 Amabile and Kramer, "The Power of Small Wins."

99 Ibid.

100 Ibid.

If you're *not* a football fan, and you find yourself dragged to a Super Bowl party, what's one of the first things that strike you about the game? *They stop and start constantly! There's so much setup, and then they move for all of ten seconds, and then we're back to setup! The ball barely moves down the field!*

I can understand this complaint—but what you're watching is the progress loop in action. Each ten yards that the team moves the ball, the announcer cheers, the crowd cheers, everyone celebrates. On and on, until they score a touchdown.

Compare this to soccer (and if you live anywhere else in the world besides the USA, I do mean football, and yes, I acknowledge the confusing nature of this section for you), where game play goes on and on and on with hardly any major celebration—just a steady low cheering, more of a *come on, you got it, let's go*—until once in a blue moon when a goal is finally scored and the stadium erupts. It's exciting, but it's not exactly a celebration of incremental progress.

There are several ways to practice the frequent recognition of progress. Here are three of my favorites:

1. **Celebrate in the moment.** We're all busy, and it's easy for leaders to register a win internally and move on to what feels like a more pressing issue. Instead, pause, and take 30 seconds to acknowledge wins—both team members' and your own.

2. **Make sharing wins a weekly agenda item.** Set aside time in a weekly team meeting to reflect on wins and share them aloud. Fridays can be a good day for this, but any day will work.

3. **Create a "Win Wall."** One of my clients designated a white-board as their "Win Wall." As people experience wins, they write them on the wall. Very big and very little wins are encouraged. People also write wins about someone else—*Zach crushed it in that board meeting!*

FIND WINS FOR EVERYONE—INCLUDING YOU

Often, people who get recognized and celebrated for wins are the ones who crossed the goal line. Going back to football (bear with me), it's the receiver in the endzone doing the touchdown dance. *Very* occasionally, the on-air announcers will spotlight the offensive lineman in the middle of the field who used every ounce of strength to prevent the quarterback from getting sacked—but usually, it's just not where your eyes go first.

In organizations, the people who did a lot of vital work to enable a team's success often get overlooked. Everybody needs the motivation—everybody needs the win.

Whenever the team reaches a collective goal, your job as a leader is to consider who else had a role beyond the obvious one or two people. Who made sure everything was accurate? Who created the document? Who supported the project in any way? Those people need to be celebrated.

Scanning for the positive and making sure people aren't overlooked are just crucial steps to keeping your team motivated. Yep, all of this applies to you, too. High achievers often keep plowing through, neglecting to notice their wins along the way. Often, they're focused on the next goal. Or, thanks to negativity bias, what could be done better.

Many of my clients don't even notice—much less celebrate—their many wins. So I ask them to email me a list of wins, big and small, from the week. It makes them reflect on what they've accomplished and receive that positive hit they need to stay motivated and productive. Navigating interpersonal issues, responding to feedback without being defensive, getting a proposal out, finalizing a budget, meeting a performance metric...these are all wins. And they all deserve to be celebrated.

BUSINESS BREAKTHROUGHS

Teams that celebrate wins report higher levels of collaboration, engagement, and productivity across the board. Motivation is so crucial to business outcomes that it impacts nearly every marker of employee engagement and success. Motivated employees are 20 percent more productive,[101] 87 percent less likely to resign,[102] and 60 percent less likely to feel stressed at work.

---

101 Camille Preston, "Promoting Employee Happiness Benefits Everyone," *Forbes*, December 13, 2017, https://www.forbes.com/sites/forbescoachescouncil/2017/12/13/promoting-employee-happiness-benefits-everyone/?sh=14fda847581a.

102 Li, "17 Surprising Statistics."

CONNECT TO THE PRESENT

In a way, celebrating wins is a practice of mindfulness.

This is where I began my work with Colin, who was, to his credit, a little mortified to learn the reason why energy on his team was so low.

"It makes sense now," he told me in our first session. "People come in to our team so fired-up and excited, but by about six to eight months in, that excitement is dulled. I get it—they're not seeing the progress they're making."

I asked him about what a win would look like on a more frequent basis, and he was stumped. "The *win* is going to market," he said. "The win is launching the product and *already* being halfway through making the next awesome version!"

Not hard to see where he was leaving his team behind. Colin wasn't just living in the future launch of the current product; he was living halfway through the future development on the next one.

We started with practices that pulled him back to the present. I wanted Colin to *be where he was*, to begin to inhabit his present moment more. In doing so, my goal was that he'd begin to see the everyday wins that added up to forward momentum.

"You're part of your team," I said. "You're not a separate entity. You're a member. So, thinking about the team you're on, what's one positive thing that happens in the space of *one day,* that is frequent enough that you could track it?"

It took some mulling over, but eventually, he landed on it: "We do a design review and push the new design revision out to engineering every week. That's a big moment for the team, because we're basing the revision on test user feedback, and we can see the product evolving toward its final form on a regular basis."

Perfect. That idea got him rolling, and as he thought of more small, incremental wins, they became even more common.

"It's a win when we even get the test user feedback in the first place."

"It's a win when the UX squad finishes a feature wireframe."

"It's a win when we have a group lunch—great ideas flow out of those lunches organically."

Colin and I worked together to create two goal models the team could track visually. One was the team's big "umbrella" goal—the two-year runway from idea to launch. This was broken out into quarterly, monthly, and weekly goals. Wins could be tracked within each increment to show progress toward the next goal line.

The other goal model was an individual goal breakdown for each member of the team, showing how their specific role impacted the team's overall umbrella goal and how their individual achievements fit into the big picture. Each team member ended up with the same quarterly, monthly, and weekly increments in which they could track their own progress.

Armed with these models, Colin went back to his team and leaned heavily into one-on-ones with his team members. He needed to do a little Platinum work right at the start to discover what individually sparked each person.

"It's incredible," he told me on a call halfway through his initial series of one-on-ones. "I would *never* have imagined the variety of things that motivate people. It's hard to wrap my head around some of them—they're so…small, normal, everyday!"

"Everyday to *you*," I reminded him. "Try to see their wins on *their* scale, not yours."

Once he had individual motivations and goal models nailed down, Colin began using a meeting format that I've coached for years: Wins, Challenges, Goals.

Wins, Challenges, Goals is a structure for meetings that covers a huge number of the concepts in this book with one simple format. The goal is to split each meeting into three sections (they don't have to be equal in timeframe—you choose how long each section is).

The first section is for Wins; each team member shares one to three wins that have happened since the last meeting. The first time you do this, you may notice that people are slightly uncomfortable, or preface their wins with statements like, "It's not a big deal or anything, but…"

This goes away after a few times breaking the ice on sharing wins, and soon they'll be excitedly pumping each other up with each win shared.

The next section is Challenges, and is usually the meat of the agenda. Team members share all the current challenges in what they're working on and offer each other help, solutions, and ideas.

The final section is Goals. This is where each team member lays out what they plan to accomplish before the next meeting, and with your guidance, everyone prioritizes what they're working on. With this structure, positivity, collaboration, and clarity are maximized across the team.

Unlike the changes in Marcus's team, which took six months to show, the changes in Colin's team were more immediate. Suddenly hearing about everyday wins, tracking them visually, and celebrating with their teammates was a huge dopamine hit to what had been a *very* dopamine-thirsty group of people. Colin's team of rockstars was, for the first time, *enjoying* their stardom. They were seeing their achievement consistently, and feeling a huge sense of progress and motivation—even though the main goalpost, two years out, hadn't moved at all.

My next call with Eleanor was a total 180 in tone.

"The energy over there is completely different!" she reported back excitedly. "For the first time, that crew is actually walking around like the A-players they are. In fact, I've got a new problem on my hands."

I asked what it was. "Well, whereas before, the morale dip was all centered around Colin's team, now it's spread to the other leaders at Colin's level. Because the number of transfer requests from people on *their* teams has skyrocketed. Everyone wants to jump ship to be on his team—and the team leads across the company are wondering what they're doing wrong!"

I chuckled as I pulled up my session calendar and made note of all the slots I'd need to open up for the rest of the team leads.

YOU GET SOLID: SELF-EVALUATION

1. Can you name five wins your team achieved last week?

2. Are you stuck, with no wins in sight? If so, how can you recalibrate your goals?

3. Are your team goals broken up into smaller ones?

4. Do you celebrate small wins or only the big ones?

5. What are some easy ways you can build celebrating wins into the way your team functions? Do you need to create a virtual "whiteboard" to record progress?

6. Are there people on your team who rarely get acknowledged? Pay special attention to their wins.

7. Can you name five wins you personally experienced this week? Would it be helpful to make this a weekly practice?

THEY GET SOLID: NEXT STEPS

1. Ask team members to jot down anything that felt like a win over the week.

2. Take ten minutes at the beginning of your weekly team meeting to share the wins aloud. See what happens.

9

PLAY

A Robert Half survey found that 91 percent of executives believe a sense of humor is important for career advancement, while 84 percent feel people with a good sense of humor do a better job.[103]

"I want to be on the *fun* team!"

No, this isn't a continuation of Eleanor's new problem from Chapter 8. Believe it or not, it's something I often hear from multiple employees at the same company. Somehow, a narrative forms among the employees that their environment is a drab, monotonous slog, and there's one particular team, one shiny castle in the clouds, that sticks out as a magical, golden happy place of fun-times and joy.

Is the rest of the office a doldrums of stress and boredom? No. Hardly ever. But the contrast of seeing one team that appears to be having the time of their lives every day at work—and you're not on it—certainly makes it feel that way.

---

103 Robert Half, "Is a Sense of Humour in the Workplace Good for Your Career?" Robert Half Talent Solutions, March 27, 2017, https://www.roberthalf.com.au/blog/jobseekers/sense-humour-workplace-good-your-career.

You can probably picture it: that one department meeting that always shakes the building with the laughter and energy in the conference room. People at their desks outside the room look up at the sound of fun happening where they're not. They crane their necks and look around. They see it shining from across the rows of desks—the glass-paneled conference room, its light illuminating the rest of the space, filled with happy people having a great time. It's like an oasis in the desert. Their own mundane situation begins to feel like trudging through molasses in comparison.

I was experiencing a version of this—but *worse*—at a large branding agency I'd been brought in to work with. I had begun by coaching the company's leadership, but within three or four sessions, I'd gleaned enough about the workplace to understand a major challenge they were facing.

There were two main account teams, each led by a VP. The teams had the same number of team members, with the same roles and responsibilities. The workload was the same. The work*flow* was the same.

And yet one was the "fun team," and the other was the "dull team."

The Fun Team—let's call them AFC Richmond—exemplified happiness. They were energetic, fulfilled; they chatted excitedly over lunch, you could hear the laughter from their group meetings across the entire floor, and their outlook was, overall, the embodiment of optimism.

Their leader VP—let's call him Ted Lasso—was, well…Ted Lasso. Human sunshine. Always a kind word, a quick joke, a funny anecdote, a "go team." Everyone on the team took his joyous spark and amplified it with their mood and behavior.

Now, the Dull Team—let's call them...

(Okay, actually, I'm not going to assign the name of an actual British football team because I've seen what the fans are like when it comes to loyalty, and I value my inbox. So, let's just call them The Other Team.)

The Other Team was the polar opposite of AFC Richmond in mood, attitude, and overall happiness. They were constantly stressed. They walked around with the weight of the world on their shoulders. They were glum, serious, tense. There was *no* spark.

Their leader VP—let's call him (...nope, after careful consideration, I won't draw any comparisons to real-life sports coaches for the same reasons) Professor Snape—was, just like the diametric opposition of the two teams, the *polar* opposite of Ted Lasso. Professor Snape was traditional. He was serious, aloof, and totally focused on getting things done. He also had a tendency to default to pessimism when obstacles arose, and his near-constant simmer of stress was contagious. His entire team reflected his dark, gloomy vibe.

The two teams had *exactly* the same number of accounts, with *exactly* the same types of challenges their clients threw at them. But every time a new challenge arose, their reactions were in different universes.

AFC Richmond: *Well, hot dang, I feel like we fell out of the lucky tree and hit every branch on the way down, ended up in a pool of cash and Sour Patch Kids!*

The Other Team: *Dealing with this client is like fighting a many-headed monster...each time a neck is severed, a new head sprouts that is even fiercer and cleverer than before...*

In the time I'd been working with the company, I had a couple of designated days per month filled with one-on-one sessions for any team members across the organization who wanted to have one. And after a month, the number of times I'd heard team members from The Other Team declare that they wanted to be on AFC Richmond was stunning.

Moreover, it was reinforcing a vicious cycle for Professor Snape. Each of his team members who ran screaming to Ted Lasso's team just stressed him out more. His mood got darker, his interactions grew more tense, the morale of his team dipped even further, and…you guessed it, more team members fled.

I did some detective work to validate that there was truly *no* difference between the teams besides the originating spark—or lack of—of their leaders.

There wasn't.

It was time for some one-on-one time, just me and Professor Snape (boy, there's a sentence I never thought I'd write). To turn the vicious cycle he and his team were caught in into a *virtuous* cycle, I needed to shift his entire outlook. I needed to help him show up completely differently, within the bounds of what would be authentic to him.

I needed to help Professor Snape bring the fun.

THE AMAZING EFFECTS OF LAUGHTER

When my husband and I hit a rough patch, we don't schedule a therapy appointment.

218

Or, we do—but it doesn't look like most people's idea of therapy. We buy tickets to a comedy club.

Spending an evening laughing together changes our whole way of interacting. We bond. We relax. We feel better about life and each other.

Laughter isn't just good for marriages—it's important in all relationships, even work ones. Or maybe, most importantly, work ones.

Many of the topics crucial to leadership and team success—authenticity, psychological safety, connection—all happen naturally in times of lightness and joy. A culture that values and incorporates levity and humor into the inherent seriousness of work is proven to foster greater outcomes, including team performance. And not just in the moment—sometimes years later!

And, you won't be surprised to learn, it begins with you.

I have a special tactic whenever a client wants to improve their public speaking. The day of their presentation, I write a joke on a sticky note. I tell my client to put it in their pocket and read it just before they go to speak.

Backstage, as soon as they laugh, their stress drops. Their cortisol levels go down, they can access their rational brain again, and they're ready to knock their presentation out of the park. They're relaxed, more themselves.

Research shows that laughter brings about the following immediate physical benefits:[104]

104 Gabriel Berezin and Mika Liss, "The Neuroscience of Laughter, and How to Inspire More of It at Work," Neuroleadership.com, September 17, 2020, https://neuroleadership.com/your-brain-at-work/neuroscience-laughter-at-work/.

- Increased endorphins, or hormones that boost feelings of pleasure

- Increased dopamine, the "feel-good" neurotransmitter

- Increased oxytocin, the "bonding" chemical that creates feelings of relatedness

- Lowered cortisol, the stress hormone

- Increased, then decreased heart rate and blood pressure, which makes you feel more relaxed

- Increased circulation

- Relaxed muscles

While all of these benefits are incredible, two stand out to me when I think about creating sparks for your team.

One is the increased dopamine. Research shows we don't just get a dopamine hit when we laugh—we begin to feel good simply at the idea, or anticipation, we might laugh.[105] It signals expected pleasure, and encourages us to seek out more. That means someone who's learned to infuse joy into their work interactions with others will be sought out for more connection.

Second, laughter gives us a hit of oxytocin—that oh-so-useful bonding chemical at work once again. Bonded teams produce results.

---

105 Kelley Colihan, "Cut Stress by Anticipating Laughter?" WebMD.com, April 7, 2008, https://www.webmd.com/balance/stress-management/news/20080407/cut-stress-by-anticipating-laughter.

Despite these proven perks, adults don't laugh nearly as much as they could. While a child laughs 300 times a day, on average, an adult laughs only seventeen times daily.[106] (Why so serious? It's a good question to ask yourself in the mirror from time to time.)

To make things even more grim, people laugh significantly less on weekdays than on the weekends, according to a Gallup survey.[107] So, not only are we a bunch of grumpy adults who laugh less than kids, it's even worse when we're at work.

It doesn't have to be that way—and teams like AFC Richmond are proof.

FUN: THE SECRET SAUCE

Confession time—Play wasn't supposed to be a chapter in this book. But then one of my clients pointed out to me how much I talk about the importance of humor and joy in happy, high-functioning teams. "You should write a blog post about fun!" he told me, and I realized he was right. Play is just as important a component of Platinum Leadership as each of the chapters you've read so far.

Fun primes our minds and bodies for better communication and connection among coworkers. It bonds us, lightens the cognitive load, builds trust, and helps us understand each other better. Fun makes the workplace feel safe, happy, and motivating.

---

106 Rod A. Martin, "Do Children Laugh Much More Often than Adults Do?" Association for Applied and Therapeutic Humor, https://aath.memberclicks.net/do-children-laugh-much-more-often-than-adults-do.

107 Alison Beard, "Leading with Humor," *Harvard Business Review*, May 2014, https://hbr.org/2014/05/leading-with-humor.

Professor and behavioral scientist Jennifer Aaker, MBA, and executive coach Naomi Bagdonas, MBA, created a popular Stanford Graduate School of Business course called "Humor: Serious Business." For six years, they ran studies involving more than 1.5 million people worldwide, pored over research, interviewed hundreds of leaders and comedians, and more.

"If there's one thing our research makes clear," they write in their 2021 book, "it's that we don't need to take ourselves so seriously in order to grapple with serious things."[108]

On the contrary, their work suggests teams that laugh together are more bonded, creative, and resilient. Their authentic connection is powerful.

Fun in Numbers

- A broad study of the effect of humor on work showed that people who are exposed to humor have a higher task completion rate.[109]

- One study showed that employee happiness leads to 20 percent higher productivity.[110]

---

108 Jennifer Aaker and Naomi Bagdonas, *Humor, Seriously: Why Humor Is a Secret Weapon in Business and Life (and How Anyone Can Harness It. Even You)* (New York: Currency, 2021), 13

109 Jessica Lindsey, "How a Little Humor Can Improve Your Work Life," *Greater Good*, October 15, 2019, https://greatergood.berkeley.edu/article/item/how_a_little_humor_can_improve_your_work_life.

110 Preston, "Promoting Employee Happiness Benefits Everyone."

- A UK study by the University of Warwick showed an average increase of 12 percent, and a high of 20 percent, in the productivity of people who watch a comedy clip before performing a task.[111]

- Employees who have a best friend at work are twice as likely to be engaged as employees who don't.[112]

- People with a positive mindset are significantly more creative than those with a negative or neutral mindset.[113]

- On a survey from the Great Place to Work Institute, which produces Fortune's 100 Best Companies to Work For list, the overwhelming majority of companies who make the "great" list get top "fun" scores from their employees.[114]

---

111 John Arenas, "Greater Happiness Leads to Greater Productivity, Study Finds," SerendipityLabs.com, https://serendipitylabs.com/greater-happiness-leads-to-greater-productivity-study-finds/.

112 Johnny Wood, "Why It's Good to Turn Your Colleagues into Friends," World Economic Forum, November 22, 2019, https://www.weforum.org/agenda/2019/11/friends-relationships-work-productivity-career/.

113 Shawn Achor, "Positive Intelligence," *Harvard Business Review*, January 2012, https://hbr.org/2012/01/positive-intelligence.

114 Adrian Gostick and Scott Christopher, "Why Fun at Work Matters," Monster.com, https://www.monster.com/career-advice/article/fun-at-work-matters-levity-effect.

In his yearlong study of professional chefs, Owen Hanley Lynch, PhD, an organizational communications professor at Southern Methodist University, found that humor among coworkers can ensure work meets the group's standards.

In a busy restaurant kitchen, there's no time for slack. Chefs play pranks on peers who aren't paying close enough attention, such as putting a pot handle in a flame when the user turns their back. Ha-ha! Also: ouch!

Managers are a common foil for chefs' humor, Lynch found in his study, published in the *Journal of Applied Communication Research*.[115] It turns out, chefs find great joy in asking managers nonsensical questions about complex cooking techniques. In a high-stress environment, this behavior eases tensions and bonds the chefs, reinforcing their shared identity.

PLAYFUL LEADERSHIP IN ACTION

Here are a few ways you, as a leader, can spark a culture that values fun.

Action #1: Set the Tone

You don't have to be a comedian. You're not funny or gregarious? No problem. All you have to do as a leader is set the bar for what's acceptable. Show people it's okay to reveal their joyful side, that their authenticity is valued and appreciated.

---

115 Owen Hanley Lynch, "Kitchen Antics: The Importance of Humor and Maintaining Professionalism at Work," *Journal of Applied Communication Research* 37, no. 4 (2009): 444–64, https://www.tandfonline.com/doi/abs/10.1080/00909880903233143.

When someone cracks a joke, laugh. When someone tells a funny story, take the time for everyone to soak it in. Yes, you've got a meeting to run, but little opportunities for bonding that bubble up during a regular workday are just as impactful as the work itself.

Action #2: Create Traditions

After a Platinum-style team evaluation, one of my CEO clients discovered that humor was a top value of many of his team members, even though they seemed like a *very* serious bunch.

He created a First Fridays tradition by crowdsourcing the group for ideas. He held up a "fun basket" (an empty basket from home) and asked his employees to write down an idea the team could do for under two hundred dollars that would be fun to them and put it in the "fun basket."

On Monday before the first Friday of every month, he'd pick a slip of paper from the basket, and that's what they would plan for the following Friday afternoon. The events didn't need to be expensive or a big deal to plan—often they were as simple as cornhole, burgers, and beer out in the parking lot.

Action #3: Spice Up Boring Tasks

Everyone has to stay late to meet an important deadline? Break the monotony and ease tensions with an ice cream bar. It's not hard or expensive—a few cartons of ice cream, some plastic bowls and spoons, a few toppings, fifteen minutes of eating, chatting, maybe laughing, and you're back to work, newly bonded and relaxed, ready to face the task anew.

Action #4: Walk and Talk

I have a client who has a weekly one-on-one meeting with a top team member in another state on the phone rather than through Zoom. *No more cameras*, they agreed.

Before they meet, they each get a fancy coffee—a treat they both enjoy but rarely indulge in. Then they slip on their headphones, walk, sip and talk.

Seems simple, but it has a big impact: it sets the understanding that joy and connection are just as important as the work itself. Plus, they're both more relaxed and open, and often end up going deeper on the discussion topics than they would have on the same old video call at their desks.

Action #5: Create a Just-For-Fun Slack Channel

Set up a Slack channel about a topic of interest, like pets, kids, favorite movies, restaurant recommendations—you name it. And as the leader, participate!

BUSINESS BREAKTHROUGHS

When it comes to profit, it might not seem like a playful, joyful, *fun* workplace would be a big needle-mover. And yet when we look at the Fortune 100 list, 81 percent of the top 100 companies in the US earn top marks on being a fun place to work.[116] That's what I call incontrovertible proof of the business ROI of fun!

---

116 Gostick and Christopher, "Why Fun at Work Matters."

FUN COMES IN MANY FORMS

"Professor Snape, what makes you laugh?"

(I swear that when I started down this metaphor road, I had no idea the extent of the comedy potential it had—at least for me.)

Professor Snape frowned—naturally—and had to think for a while. We were in an in-person session at his office. I'd explained what I'd seen in the morale and attitude of the two teams, and how I felt the biggest needle to move was truly *him,* and the spark he was providing his team.

Finally, he looked me dead in the eye, and said, "GIFs."

Huh?

Part of the problem was that he pronounced it with a soft G, like the peanut butter, and I, like all reasonable people, pronounce it with a hard G.

"GIFs? Like, the little video things you send people?" I asked.

He nodded. "They crack me up." No further explanation.

"Okay," I said. "I mean, GIFs are definitely a primary mode of communication online—I've had text conversations with friends that are just GIF exchanges that go on for months. Have you ever, say, slacked a GIF to someone on your team in response to something they said? That could be a way to inject some levity into the conversation."

My primary goal with Professor Snape was to get the lighter side of his personality showing—but in a way that was authentic to him, and didn't feel forced. There was no way we were going to turn Professor Snape into Ted Lasso, and we would never want to, because the lack of authenticity would damage the trust and connection he had with his team.

It turned out that Snape didn't know about the /giphy extension on Slack. I showed it to him, in a mildly surreal reversal of roles—it's usually other people, like my kids, showing *me* the current online trends.

That was the start of a slow but sure change in the vibe of The Other Team. Once Professor Snape had the wide world of GIFs at his fingertips on Slack, he put it to good use. And it turned out that Snape wasn't just a connoisseur of funny GIFs—he was a comedian in his own right. Over the weeks after that session, I began to hear from Other Team members about his perfectly timed, perfectly curated GIF responses that turned what were once dull or tense conversations into subtle hilarity. It was dark humor, but it was humor, and the whole team started to get into it.

Rome wasn't built in a day, and The Other Team didn't turn into AFC Richmond overnight—in fact, they're still in pretty high contrast to each other. But the simple injection of *fun* into the life of the team completely transformed their outlook. People began to loosen up, crack jokes, share anecdotes, and most importantly, see the bear far less often. The contrast now is more like chocolate and vanilla, two different flavors of the same great thing.

And all it took was a little fun. (And GIF is pronounced with a hard G. Just so we're clear.)

YOU GET SOLID: SELF-EVALUATION

1. Think about times you laughed or had fun at work. What happened?

2. Throughout your day, notice what brings you the most joy. How can you insert more of that into your workday?

3. If you had a half hour each day carved out for "playtime" with your team, how would you spend it?

4. In your next presentation, add two relevant memes or GIFs.

5. Choose an upcoming meeting to take outside on a walk-and-talk.

THEY GET SOLID: NEXT STEPS

1. Start a "fun" committee at work. Anyone can join. Set a budget that is 100 percent committed to the team spending time together simply having fun.

2. Find opportunities to gamify common team tasks. Create friendly competition with rewards for the winners.

3. Schedule a regular weekly block of time devoted to a playful activity that builds connection on Slack, Teams, or wherever your team does most of their communication. A GIF-off, a Photo Friday...even just a half hour of digital play built into the workday allows the team to build camaraderie and play.

10

PRACTICE

A five-minute daily gratitude journal can increase your long-term well-being by more than 10 percent—the same impact as doubling your income.[117]

"It was all going so well...*what happened?*"

Pradeep, a VP of Product who normally had a serene energy, was anything but calm on our session that day. As soon as he'd signed in to the Teams window, I knew something had shaken him. He'd been acting a little off for weeks—I'd noticed an overall dip in confidence, and even a slight nervousness that was unlike him.

Today, he'd started out immediately with his bad news.

"The team is officially back to where they were a year ago," he told me. "They're low energy and their productivity has plummeted, but at the same time, they're claiming they're burned out. A few of them have disengaged entirely."

---

117 "31 Benefits of Gratitude: The Ultimate Science-Backed Guide," Happier Human, August 1, 2020, https://www.happierhuman.com/benefits-of-gratitude/.

He rubbed his face with his hands, and even through the slightly grainy webcam, I could see the dark circles under his eyes. "Somehow, somewhere, I went backwards. What did I do wrong?"

Pradeep and I had been working together for over a year when his company brought me in to coach during an acquisition. He had inherited a team from the acquired company, a team that brought with them a profoundly broken culture. Pradeep had had his work cut out for him.

In the past year of Platinum Leadership, we'd built a new culture within his team, brick by brick. Pradeep had put each new element into practice carefully, and had especially put the work in on authentic connection, an area where the incoming team suffered most.

It had been an enormous period of growth for Pradeep, and he was proud of the success he saw. His team had found their spark.

Or so he thought.

After a downturn at the company, rumors of layoffs were in the air. If Pradeep had been working to spark brilliance, this sparked the exact *opposite*—everyone had begun sliding back into old habits.

"They're back to the gossip, the missed deadlines, the distrust," he recounted for me, like reading off a grocery list of bad vibes. "A lot of the pieces we worked to put in place are there functionally, but it's like no one's heart is in it. There's no optimism."

His voice was heavy, and I could tell he was taking the team's backslide as a personal failure.

"You put all the pieces in place to spark brilliance, but how did you *practice* it?" I asked him.

He looked at me blankly. "I'm not sure what you mean."

"It sounds like your team had begun to show up with optimism, to change the way they scan their environment. But just like anything else that's new, you have to practice it in order for it to change your behavior. And in this case, we're not just changing how people *act*; we're changing how people *think*."

NEUROPLASTICITY: CHANGE YOUR LENS, CHANGE YOUR BRAIN

I have a friend who just can't get on board with her teenage daughter's taste in music.

"I want to connect with her, and I want to like what she likes," she often tells me when we meet up for coffee. "I've tried to listen to it, but...I just don't get it! There's no discernable melody. There's no hook. There aren't even *instruments*. It's just computer sounds strung together in a mishmash for four minutes. It's just...*noise*."

In moments like these, we laugh, but the laughter has a tinge of self-aware horror. It's a bittersweet inevitability that despite our best efforts, we all really do turn into our parents in the end. After all, we heard exactly the same thing about *our* music when we were teenagers. *Shut that noise off!* Sound familiar?

A few years ago, a study was released that seemed to explain why my friend can't get on board with the likes of Post Malone, and why back in my day, my parents thought Guns N' Roses was mindless cacophony. The study compiled data from music streaming services, analyzed the data, and found that people generally stop discovering new music right around the same age: thirty-three.

Yup, at the ripe old age of thirty-three, your music tastes are fully baked. You lose the drive to seek out new genres and artists. "For the average listener," the study concludes, "by their mid-thirties, their tastes have matured, and they are who they're going to be."[118]

Well, that's bleak, isn't it?

I get such a kick out of reading studies like these, studies that "prove" that you can't teach an old dog new tricks, that we're all just Jell-O waiting to fully set in our molds. I find it so entertaining because I simply don't believe it to be true. And the idea that our brains are capable of adaptation only up to a certain age goes against years of scientific evidence, as well as what I've observed in my work. I've known people who have been completely set in their Jell-O molds, and with simple shifts in perspective and behavior, have completely changed their outlook. Not only that, but they've been able to create lasting change in their lives and the lives of other people simply by shifting the way they think about the world.

They no longer have to *think about* thinking differently—they just *do*. They've changed their brains.

---

118 Ajay Kalia, "Why Do We Listen to Less Pop Music as We Get Older?" *Newsweek*, May 9, 2015, https://www.newsweek.com/why-do-we-listen-less-pop-music-we-get-older-329805#:~:text=And%20for%20the%20average%20listener%2C%20by%20their%20mid-30s%2C,teens%2C%20from%20artists%20with%20a%20lower%20popularity%20rank.

This is the concept of neuroplasticity: that brains have the ability to adapt, and that our environments impact this adaptation.

Up through the mid-twentieth century, our understanding of the human brain rested on the theory that only children and adolescents, with their growing and developing brains, are capable of changes in brain structure and function—their brains are "plastic."

But in the years since, countless studies have demonstrated adult neuro-plasticity as well. For example, a recent study by neuroscientist Elea-nor Maguire of University College London found that the hippocampi of aspiring London cab drivers over a four-year period physically grew larger than a control group over the same period.[119]

The reason? Unlike more modern, grid-based cities like New York, London's 2,000-year-old city map is famously labyrinthine and dense, with clusters of tangled and knotted streets spilling out over a comparatively gigantic 607 square miles. To master every route, traffic pattern, and tourist spot requires a volume of learning over the course of several years that, as it turns out, *physically changes* the structure of taxi drivers' brains.

Adult brains can not only learn new things, they can change and rebuild their structures, for better or worse.

This creates an enormous opportunity. By changing our environment and our behavior, and by choosing to think differently, we are able to form new connections and pathways in the brain. We are able to fundamentally change how we see and react to the world.

---

119 Ferris Jabr, "Cache Cab: Taxi Drivers' Brains Grow to Navigate London's Streets," *Scientific American*, December 8, 2011, https://www.scientificamerican.com/article/london-taxi-memory/.

I recently completed a program at MIT Sloan School of Management called "Neuroscience for Business." The program was taught by Dr. Tara Swart, an inspiring doctor, neuroscientist, executive coach, and author whose work focuses on using neuroplasticity to your advantage to optimize your brain for success. In a recent article in the *Stanford Social Innovation Review*, she writes:

> Change starts with us. An understanding of how the brain works, raising from non-conscious to conscious the drivers of our behavior that may be barriers to success; priming the brain to notice and grasp opportunities that may otherwise have passed us by; turning "lack" thinking into abundance; and manifesting the real-world outcomes that we desire for ourselves and future generations, leads to a cascade effect of health, wealth (in whatever form that may be), and well-being. Key relationships are improved, and people are inspired. This is where science meets spirituality—a powerful combination that can reap benefits for all.[120]

When I hear from a client like Pradeep that he's "gone backwards," what immediately clicks in my head is: *A-ha! He changed his behavior, but he didn't actually change how he thinks. His lens is still the same; he didn't change his brain.*

Just like the trombone your mom made you practice back in middle school (or insert whatever unwieldy rented musical instrument you lugged around in a beat-up case), getting good at Platinum requires practicing it over and over.

---

120   Tara Swart, "The Neuroscience of Creativity," *Stanford Social Innovation Review*, October 11, 2019, https://ssir.org/books/excerpts/entry/the_neuroscience_of_creativity.

So *how* do you practice it? How do you practice the way you show up in the world? How do you practice this new way of thinking—optimistic, solution-focused, and constantly scanning for the positive, rather than seeing the bear everywhere you look?

The answer is simple: gratitude.

Gratitude has such a strong effect because it trains your brain to focus on the positive. Feelings of gratitude activate our favorite feel-good brain chemical, dopamine. You know how dopamine works by now: when you get a rush of it, you're motivated to repeat the action that caused it. In this case, it's practicing gratitude that causes a virtuous cycle.

Robert A. Emmons, professor of psychology at the University of California, Davis, and a leading researcher on the science of gratitude, suggests through his research[121] that people who keep regular gratitude lists are more likely to:

- Experience positive physical effects, such as fewer ailments

- Feel more optimistic about the upcoming week

- Make progress toward important personal goals

- Feel alert, enthusiastic, and attentive

- Help someone with a personal problem or offer emotional support

---

121   Robert A. Emmons, "Why Gratitude Is Good," Greater Good, November 16, 2010, https://greatergood.berkeley.edu/article/item/why_gratitude_is_good.

Additionally, depression symptoms ease the more grateful a person becomes, another effect uncovered by a group of Chinese researchers.[122] They studied gratitude as it relates to insomnia and anxiety, as well. Good news: being thankful leads to better sleep and, as a result, less anxiety.

Gratitude in Numbers

- Seventy-five percent of job success is predicted by levels of optimism, social support, and ability to see stress as a challenge instead of a threat.[123]

- Eighty-eight percent of people say that expressing gratitude to colleagues makes them feel happier and more fulfilled.[124]

- Four in five (81 percent) employees report they are motivated to work harder when their boss shows appreciation for their work.[125]

---

122 Hongyu Liang et al., "Mediating Effects of Peace of Mind and Rumination on the Relationship Between Gratitude and Depression among Chinese University Students," Springer Link, April 14, 2018, https://link.springer.com/article/10.1007/s12144-018-9847-1.

123 Shawn Achor, "The Happiness Advantage: Linking Positive Brains to Performance," June 30, 2011, TEDxBloomington, https://www.youtube.com/watch?v=GXy__kBVq1M.

124 Barbara Palmer, "How to Express Gratitude at Work," PCMA.org, November 21, 2017, https://www.pcma.org/gratitude-workplace/.

125 Ibid.

- When employees receive recognition for doing good work, 83 percent report a more positive employee experience. When workers don't receive recognition, only 38 percent have a positive experience.[126]

- Companies that invest just 1 percent of payroll into social recognition programs show an average increase in employee productivity of $1,737 per employee.[127]

My husband, sons, and I are gratitude enthusiasts. Every night, we share three things we're grateful for. We're specific, but the topics vary—making a new friend, turning in a history paper, going to In-N-Out for animal style fries. Or sometimes the topics are more profound, like "We helped a friend through a hard time" or "I'm grateful Papa's cancer treatments are working." We've done our "gratitude share" for twelve years, no misses. If someone's not home for it, we FaceTime them, or they send a text to the family group with their gratefuls in advance. And we have no plans to stop because we all, even my boys, like the way it makes us feel too much. It ends our day on a note of connection. It lowers our stress, helps us learn new things about each other's days and perspectives, and

---

126 Sarah Payne, "Workhuman Analytics and Research Institute and IBM Smarter Workforce Institute Unveil a New Employee Experience Index," Workhuman, October 4, 2016, https:// www.workhuman.com/resources/globoforce-blog/globoforce-workhuman-research-institute-and-ibm-smarter-workforce-institute-unveil-a-new-employee-experience-index.

127 Aaron Kinne, "The Human Workplace: Good for Humans, Good for Business," Workhuman, May 11, 2021, https://www.workhuman.com/resources/globoforce-blog/the-human-workplace-good-for-humans-good-for-business.

keeps us scanning for the positive. As a result, every day, just moving through our lives, we notice things that make us happy and thankful. All. The. Time.

Your team can feel the same.

THE SIMPLE POWER OF "THANK YOU"

Former Campbell's CEO Douglas Conant began sending thank-you notes early in his career. He appreciated those who supported him after he was unexpectedly fired, and he wrote to let them know. He discovered his gesture meant something to recipients, and he decided to keep the practice up during his years leading several organizations.

At last count, he'd written more than 30,000 notes to people at every level, in nearly every department.

"The notes celebrate specific achievements and contributions," writes Conant in his *Conant Leadership* blog. "It shows I'm paying attention. And that I'm deeply grateful."[128]

Practicing gratitude brings extreme benefits, as discussed above. But being appreciated and recognized for the valuable experiences you provide at the workplace has important benefits, too—one too many leaders overlook.

---

128 Douglas R. Conant, "10 Powerful Ways to Give Thanks with Your Leadership," Conant Leadership, November 22, 2017, https://conantleadership.com/10-powerful-ways-to-give-thanks-leadership/.

About half of employees say they are thanked less than once a week by their supervisor, according to researchers at USC Marshall School of Business. Colleagues do a better job of showing gratitude to one another—nearly three-quarters say they're thanked by coworkers at least once a week.[129]

People need to hear it, Conant contends. It's as simple as that. A paycheck simply isn't enough to feel understood and valued, to build relationships, and to have a happy, productive team.

Showing gratitude isn't just the right thing to do—it also boosts performance. Researchers at the Wharton School at the University of Pennsylvania divided fundraisers into two groups. One group made calls to solicit donations from alumni as usual. The other group first received a pep talk from the annual director of giving, who said she was grateful for their efforts. The group that heard from the director made 50 percent more fundraising calls the following week than the other group.[130]

When you start scanning for the positive and savoring it when you find it, you'll notice opportunities and seize them. Psychologists call this "predictive encoding." Priming yourself to expect a favorable outcome encodes the brain to recognize the outcome when it arises. When you're armed with positivity, your brain stays open to possibility.

---

129   Jenesse Miller, "Many Employees Feel Underappreciated at Work and Would Like a 'Thank You' More Often," USCNews.edu, November 19, 2020, https://news.usc.edu/179031/underappreciated-employees-thank-you-at-work-bosses-usc-research/.

130   Ruth Umoh, "How Being Thankful Can Boost Your Well-Being and Success, According to Science," CNBC.com, November 22, 2017, https://www.cnbc.com/2017/11/22/how-being-thankful-can-boost-your-well-being-and-success.html.

A GRATEFUL WORKPLACE

I find focusing on gratitude is an especially useful tactic when I'm working with a team that's super stressed and, for lack of a better phrase, falling apart.

One of my longtime CEO clients asked me to work with a group she'd tasked with overhauling a major section of the business. The deadlines were demanding, she knew, but not impossible. Yet the group was making mistakes and seriously behind.

When I met with the group, I sensed the tension right away. They were short with one another and seemed quick to deflect responsibility.

"I'm not even sure the underlying hypothesis behind this project makes sense," one of the project managers said within the first ten minutes. (Well, if that ain't a *glowing* review…)

I decided to work with the team first on how they were showing up for the project—and for each other.

I gave a quick rundown on gratitude and its effects, emphasizing the "easy" and "powerful" parts. Then I set a gratitude challenge: Everyone had to send their coworkers a daily text with three things they were grateful for.

The responses trickled in at first, but quickly began to build. If someone was slow to send their grati-text, others reminded them. Not only did they hold each other accountable, they built stronger connections.

One man, Richard, noted he was grateful a group of boys invited his son to play basketball. Everyone on that team happened to be a parent, and each could relate to the heartbreaking feeling when your child is excluded and the elation that comes when someone reaches out. Richard sometimes demanded more from his coworkers than they thought necessary. But seeing his parental concern and gratitude helped the team warm to him. Authentic connection—it wins *every time!*

Appreciation for coworkers was a popular grati-text topic, too. As the days passed, I noticed more support, less stress, and even some laughter among the group.

The impact of gratitude in reducing stress is downright predictable. I challenge people in this way all the time. If someone is stressed about something—if they're about to give a presentation, for instance—I'll ask them to fire off three things they're grateful for. When they stop to consider the question, they relax. They simply can't be grateful and stressed simultaneously.

As Alex Korb notes in his book *The Upward Spiral: Using Neuroscience to Reverse the Course of Depression, One Small Change at a Time,* a person who worries too much about adverse outcomes "will subconsciously rewire his brain to process negative information only."[131] But by consciously practicing gratitude, we train our brains to focus on positive emotions and thoughts, reducing anxiety and feelings of apprehension.

And, through the magic of neuroplasticity—we can actually *change our brains* through practicing gratitude. Our brains learn to focus on the positive. We learn to stop seeing the bear behind every corner. Instead, we only see the bear when he actually rears his toothy head.

---

131 Alex Korb, *The Upward Spiral: Using Neuroscience to Reverse the Course of Depression, One Small Change at a Time* (Oakland: New Harbinger Publications, Inc., 2015).

BUSINESS BREAKTHROUGHS

Dr. Emmons once called gratitude "the ultimate performance-enhancing substance."[132] When you invest in a gratitude practice in your organization, it impacts not only the receivers of the gratitude, but the givers as well. The impact on business outcomes is huge due to increased motivation, collaboration, and retention. Companies with a strong gratitude practice stand to earn an additional $26 million in revenue per year simply due to the power of giving and receiving thanks.[133]

GRATITUDE IN ACTION

Here's the action plan to begin practicing gratitude with your team—and solidify the practice of all the hard work you've put in to spark brilliance.

Action #1: Start with Gratitude

Some leaders end their meetings with a round of gratitude, but I like setting the tone by showing appreciation before diving into the agenda.

---

132 Aaron Kinne, "Gratitude–the Ultimate Performance-Enhancing Substance," Workhuman, March 27, 2019, https://www.workhuman.com/resources/globoforce-blog/gratitude-the-ulti-mate-performance-enhancing-substance.

133 Eric Mosley, "The ROI of Gratitude in the Workplace," McGraw Hill Business Blog, June 19, 2019, https://mcgrawhillprofessionalbusinessblog.com/2019/06/19/the-roi-of-gratitude-in-the-workplace/.

Like Michelle Gielan's Power Lead technique we discussed earlier, not only does it inspire more positive meetings, but it also gives gratitude practice its due respect. Focusing on what we're thankful for has so many benefits, as you've read—it shouldn't be put off to the end and rushed.

Action #2: Gratitude Jar

I like to find an interesting vessel for this one—some sort of jar that's clearly not an office supply. Next to it, place embossed cards and a nice pen. (Sure, plain ol' scraps of paper or index cards work, too, but there's something compelling about specialty stationery.)

When the notion strikes, team members write what they're grateful for and put it in the jar. At the end of the week, the messages are read aloud at a meeting or a casual hangout.

The gratitude jar creates an opportunity to show appreciation for someone who helped you out of a jam or put in some extra hours to finish a task. Or, you can call out someone who routinely does great work and is dependable, kind, or funny.

Action #3: Gratitude Wall

We've talked about Win Walls, which are goal- and progress-focused. Gratitude walls are similar, but their purpose is to allow people to create a highly visible reminder of the power of being thankful. You can also set up an electronic version of this on a gratitude-focused Slack channel. Whenever someone needs a pick-me-up, they can read what their coworkers appreciate or add their own item to the list.

Action #4: Icebreaker

One of my favorite icebreakers is to go around and have everyone share something they're grateful for. It's that simple. It's a great way to shift the mood from stressed or distracted to focused and positive. Plus, it helps people learn more about one another, which strengthens authentic connections.

Action #5: Group Gratitude Text

This exercise is best for smaller teams (ideally, five or less) who agree to opt in to a twenty-one-day gratitude challenge. For three weeks, each person sends a daily text to the group, sharing three things they're grateful for.

I tend to leave it open, allowing people to choose how much they want to share or how vulnerable they want to be. It shouldn't be too hard, because one of the best things about practicing gratitude is how easy it is. And no matter how deep people go, results happen. People are happier, more helpful, and less stressed.

Key Concept: Choice

Positive Psychology gets us thinking about and taking action on all the numbers to the right of zero—the endless positive line of flourishing that represents our potential performance, satisfaction, and fulfillment.

Getting into the positive numbers, though, doesn't happen by accident. It also doesn't happen by itself. It happens by *choice*.

The positive numbers represent a shift in perspective, a move toward greater optimism and not just hope, but *confidence*, in a positive future. That shift in perspective isn't the outcome of random changes in our environment. In fact, without the element of choice, of *choosing* how we're going to perceive circumstances, changes to our environment create less of an impact than you'd think.

I see this effect all the time in corporations with deeply pessimistic, disengaged, demotivated cultures. These companies try to improve employee engagement and optimism by bringing in "culture theater": happy hours, foosball tables, Taco Tuesday, and the like. These are largely meaningless perks that do nothing to get to the root of employee dissatisfaction, and they almost never work as expected. Employees with a negative outlook will only shift their perspective when they *choose* to. Work environments that offer little in the way of connection, authenticity, meaningful relationships, celebrated wins, and demonstrated excellence create little motivation to choose an optimistic perspective.

We all, every moment, with every interaction, are subconsciously choosing how we're going to react. We're choosing our perspective. For most people, this happens without them noticing or understanding that a choice is taking place—a large contributor to the notion that the way you *perceived* something is the way it *happened*.

But it wasn't. It was how you, through the filter of every past experience that has crafted your mindset, *chose* to see it.

You have the power to choose your perception of everything around you. In a way, this is a power to choose your reality—because what we call "reality" is simply our perception of circumstances.

You can choose optimism.

You can choose happiness.

You can choose empathy and generous intent.

When you choose a positive perspective, you create decision-making and interactions that move you in the direction of a positive outcome. The acceptance of *choice* as the driving factor in our reality is what truly drives Positive Psychology—by understanding our own responsibility for our choices in each moment, we're able to take advantage of opportunities we didn't see before, sparks of potential that were previously hidden. We're able to see the positive numbers stretch even further to the right.

Paul Coelho's *The Alchemist* illustrates this concept beautifully:

> Making a decision was only the beginning of things. When someone makes a decision, he is really diving into a strong

current that will carry him to places he had never dreamed of when he first made the decision.[134]

A DAILY PRACTICE, A POSITIVE FUTURE

"Pradeep, I have good news," I told him after he'd gotten through the doom-and-gloom brainstorm he needed to get out of his system.

"Good, because if you'd told me you had *bad* news, I might have faked a bad internet connection right back," he replied, getting a genuine, and sympathetic, laugh out of me.

"All good news here. You didn't backslide. Your team still has their spark. And you still have everything you need to continue building them up."

He looked dubious. "I'm listening," he said.

I talked him through the concept of *practice.* Together, we worked out a few quick practices Pradeep could put in place with his team immediately—practices that, hopefully, would shift back to the positive numbers how people were choosing to scan and show up.

Getting Pradeep's buy-in on gratitude required a little more than this, however. He wasn't initially convinced. "I just don't see how that's going

---

134   Paul Coelho, *The Alchemist* (New York: HarperTorch, 1988, English translation) 70.

to reverse the reversal," he said glumly. "I don't see how it's going to make that big of a difference."

"Fair enough," I said. "So let's back up a second. It begins with you."

I asked Pradeep to try a personal gratitude practice for one week. That was all—the six days between our sessions. To keep it simple for him, I took a page from the book of one of my Positive Psychology mentors, Shawn Achor (of whom I am a *superfan*).

Shawn, who wrote *The Happiness Advantage,* prescribes the following daily gratitude practices:

1. **Two-Minute Gratitude Journal:** Hitting a deadline at work, having a good talk with your mom, walking in nature...whatever it is, commit to writing about a positive experience every day. With this approach, you're actually reliving the experience as you write it out. Your brain doesn't know the difference between journaling and experiencing, so it's as if the event you're grateful for has happened twice, making its effect on your brain even greater. (When a group of patients with multiple sclerosis did this exercise, they were able to reduce their pain medications by an average of 50 percent!)

2. **Text Appreciations:** Each day, text or email a different person to tell them something you appreciate about them. When you do this, the person often responds with appreciation for your thoughts, and this fills you up in turn. The

best part about this approach is its cascading effect. Your gratitude ripples and ripples, because the people you reach out to are likely to experience a shift in their own outlook as well.

I sent Pradeep off into his week with those two simple practices, and a week later, on our next call, he was bubbling with enthusiasm—back to the normally optimistic personality I'd come to know.

"*I get it now,*" he said. "When you say practice, you literally mean *practice*. Like practicing a sport or a musical instrument. When I did the gratitude practice this past week, I noticed that the way I was seeing things changed just a couple days in. My brain was naturally defaulting to the positive more."

He had changed the way he chose to show up—and he had started to see his own neuroplasticity kick in as a result. He was changing his brain.

With this demonstrated success in hand, Pradeep eagerly put in place an ongoing gratitude practice with his team. Slowly but surely, as the weeks went on, I saw the confidence come back into his demeanor. I watched his lens refocus on the positive numbers. His team swung back toward the connected, communicating, winning culture they'd built over the past year.

Practice makes—well, not *perfect*. We're not aiming for perfection. We always have more room to grow; there's no endpoint to our spark.

Practice doesn't make perfect. Practice makes *Platinum*.

YOU GET SOLID: SELF-EVALUATION

1. What are you most grateful for at work? How can you express that gratitude in a way that will spark a gratitude practice for your team?

2. Keep a two-minute gratitude journal for one week and reflect on your outlook. How has it impacted the way you scan your environment?

THEY GET SOLID: NEXT STEPS

1. In your next one-on-one meetings with team members, begin with expressing your gratitude for each of them individually. Ask them to pass on an expression of gratitude to another team member after the meeting.

2. Maintain a digital Gratitude Wall by creating a gratitude-focused Slack channel where team members are encouraged to share their gratitude practice. You can use this channel to facilitate a twenty-one-day Group Gratitude Text as well.

CONCLUSION

"It begins with me."

Lauren and I were having lunch together recently out on a sunny patio in downtown Denver. Whenever a client of mine is in town, I make it a point to take them out and connect face to face, and I'd been thrilled to get a text from Lauren the week before: *I'm headed to your hometown! Let's meet up!*

Over mimosas and a spectacular hummus plate, Lauren had been catching me up on all things Platinum. She'd worked hard in the year since her "dark time," as she called it, and her team was the proof.

Collaboration, innovation, trust, fun, optimism, performance...they'd all exploded thanks to the Platinum Leadership she'd been living. Her company had been the happy beneficiary, too; productivity and speed to market had made huge improvements, and client satisfaction ratings were through the roof. Internally, employees buzzed about the "great company culture" and how close they were with their teammates.

Lauren had even been inspired to share what she'd learned. Recently, she'd begun onboarding and developing the next incoming class of company leaders, using the Platinum Leadership methodology as a guide and practice.

She recounted all these successes to me excitedly. She was grinning, eyes sparkling—it was a total 180 from the woman who'd broken down in tears a year before, who had felt so hopeless and burned out. Lauren had a recharged energy that radiated happiness.

And then she said it. *It begins with me.*

My jaw fell open—thankfully, I was in between bites—at the natural nonchalance with which she dropped the phrase.

My heart jumped in my chest. I felt like cheering. *She's got it!*

Lauren continued on, not noticing how thrilled I was. The phrase wasn't something she'd had to dig around for, nor did it sound like she was just parroting what I'd told her in her breakthrough session last year.

No, this was different. It had come from her organically. Lauren *believed* those words. She was living them. With every moment, thought, and action, she was living Platinum Leadership.

As we were finishing up lunch, Lauren said, "By the way, how many open spots do you have on your calendar? All the new leaders I'm working with now are going to need time with you."

I felt my own happy glow spread through me, like the warmth from a campfire.

This was my spark. I was seeing it in Lauren, and now I would see it in the people Lauren had sparked in turn.

It began with me.

"I'll start blocking off some time!" I told her as we walked out to the street.

Lauren had called a rideshare to take her back to her hotel. I waited with her outside the cafe in the summer sunshine. We chatted as she kept an eye on the approaching ride on her phone, connecting over stories of our kids' summer vacation adventures.

Suddenly, looking down at her phone, she laughed hard enough that she stopped in the middle of a sentence.

"What is it?" I asked, giggling infectiously. That old emotional contagion, having its way with us yet again...

"Oh, it's just this group text I have with some friends," she told me. "We found this quiz that tells you what breed of dog you are. The answers we're all getting are *spot on*. It's cracking me up."

Her ride arrived, and she waved at the driver, then gave me a hug goodbye.

"I'll send it to you!" she told me. "It'll make your day!"

As the car pulled away from the curb and down the street away from me, my grin couldn't have been wider.

It already did.

FROM ONE SPARK TO FIREWORKS

Some of my most cherished memories of my two sons are memories of the Fourth of July.

Each year, we travel to Sun Valley, Idaho (one of our epic road trips) to be with family. It's a special day filled with fun, barbeque, and the simple joys of relaxing together in the sunshine; it was always the favorite holiday of my cousin, Kelley, to whom this book is dedicated.

As the afternoon winds down into evening and the pesky mosquitos start to come out, we can hear *booms* erupting above us; the nearby resort puts on a spectacular fireworks show. Competing with the colorful explosions overhead is the smaller, but no less spectacular, fireworks show put on by Rob, who always eagerly takes the opportunity to buy a stockpile of fireworks as we pass through Wyoming (where it's legal) on our drive up. I can usually be found nervously fake-smiling from the sidelines as Rob sets off Roman candles, rockets, helicopters, and firecrackers, each new *bang* prompting delighted cheering from the family and friends populating the small audience of spectators.

My favorite memories from these gatherings are of my kids when they were young and we'd pull out and light the sparklers. The boys were absolutely mesmerized by the pop and sizzle of the chemical reaction as the wick burned down.

The golden glow on their faces in the dark, and the pure joy with which they'd run around waving their sparklers, painting light pictures, is just about as good as it gets in life.

When I think of Platinum Leadership, my mind's eye immediately goes to those sparklers.

As the leader, you represent the single sparkler, its golden sparks flying off in all directions and illuminating the dark for your team.

The energy and power of that spark has the potential to set off a cascade.

Buddha said it best:

Thousands of flames can be lighted from a single candle, and the life of the candle will not be shortened.

You have it in you to create the brilliance you want to see in your team, simply by choosing to do so. With your spark, you can set off a whole fireworks show.

THE DEFINITION OF HAPPY

Years ago, during the study I did with children on their definition of happiness—the one with the boy who told me happiness to him was playing video games on a bed made of gold—I got one response from a ten-year-old girl that absolutely blew me away.

She wrote:

> *I looked up the definition of happy and it said cheery, excited, and joyfull. I totally agree with that but I want to add more. Being happy is diferent for everyone, just like finger prints no one has the same*

one. For exsample some things that make me happy are family, friends, soccer, candy, recess, and lots more, but what makes you happy is probly diferent. This is my definition of happy.

Kids…they're eerily smart sometimes, aren't they?

I've kept this little girl's handwritten definition of happy for almost a decade. I pull it out often, reading and rereading the subtle genius on the page, deeply fulfilled by its message.

I love the idea that happiness is defined by its indefinability.

Happiness is unique to each of us. There's no labeling it, constraining its boundaries, putting it in a box. There's no right or wrong to happiness. It only exists as the full spectrum of the way each of us feels it, as individuals.

Happiness *is* Platinum.

Each person has their own view of it, like a view of the moon that changes night by night, never the same way twice. Happiness always looks like something new through the ever-changing lens of our lives.

As a leader, your job *isn't* to make people happy.

Your job is to lead. To nurture, to inspire…to spark brilliance.

But isn't it nice to know that, in engaging in Platinum Leadership, in seeking to discover the way each person wants to be treated, you might also stumble upon what makes them happy?

I like to think that's why we were drawn to leadership in the first place. Deep down, part of what makes *us* happy is connecting with people. Understanding them. *Knowing* them.

With the methods and practices you've learned in this book, you have a whole toolkit for knowing people. You have a framework for building connection, fulfillment, and joy that will ripple outward far beyond what you yourself can see.

You have what you need to create the spark.

Begin.

Be brilliant.

ACKNOWLEDGMENTS

To be honest, writing this acknowledgments section felt really awkward. I'm not accepting an award; there's no Grammy, Nobel prize or standing ovation waiting for me when you get to the end of this book. A lot of people write books. It felt like I was trying to fake an award when there wasn't one, and that seemed a bit cringy. So, in typical Jackie fashion, I procrastinated. That was until my rock star editor, Meghan, pinged me for the tenth time reminding me of the deadline. I have counted my blessings, countless times, for Meghan's partnership and brilliance.

Then, I read my manuscript again and I had another "duh" moment. I realized that authentic connection, celebrating wins (and believe me, this is a big win for me!), and expressing gratitude are not just what I teach, but what I believe. And since this is apparently a section of the book that has "no rules," I decided to turn this into an opportunity (see, walking the walk!).

*So, I'm writing this **not** because I feel I deserve to give a thank you speech, but because I have the opportunity to genuinely thank a few people that I am so incredibly grateful for in a format that is permanent—and **that** feels awesome.*

HERE GOES:

My Clients

My Inspiration.

I am so humbled and grateful for all of you amazing leaders that allow me to serve you. It is my honor and privilege to partner with you on your journey from great to extraordinary. I learn from *you* every day, and I thank you for trusting me (even when I suggest some bizarre strategies to try), sharing with me, laughing with me, crying with me, stretching with me, and letting me share your stories in this book with other leaders who are looking to spark brilliance in their own teams. It is because of *you* that my spark is lit every day.

And an extra special thank you to my incredible mentors and the exceptional leaders who endorsed *Spark Brilliance*. Your support means the world to me, and your enthusiasm and positive feedback made a very vulnerable process flip from scary to exciting (well, mostly ;)) Thank you for sharing your brilliance with me.

My Support

My Scaffold.

To some very special people who have been my scaffold—*helping me reach new heights with the safety to do so*—I feel so blessed to share a journey with you.

My lifelong girlfriends and my sister, who embody the words "women lifting women." To truly be *seen,* without judgement, and supported and celebrated for your whole self is a gift that I will never take for granted. (Karen, Eliza, Diana, and Jen, you set the bar here.)

The family I grew up with and the family I married into, how lucky am I!?! We get to have a whole "team" of good people who are so generous, so loyal, so loving, and always put family first. What an incredible way to go through life.

(And Mom, I still aspire to be a mom like you when I grow up.)

My incredibly talented publishing team, *especially* Meghan McCracken, without whom this book would still be a gazillion ideas spinning around in my head.

I am so incredibly grateful for you all.

Rob

My Person.

I've loved you since the day I met you. I am forever grateful for your unwavering belief in me (and for keeping me laughing for twenty years). You continually show me that you see my true spark, and the light you see in me is so much bigger and brighter than I have ever seen in myself. Your pure, selfless, and loving encouragement has given me the confidence and joy to pursue my passions and be more courageous than I had thought possible. It began with you.

Simon and Miles

My Sunshine.

You two are just the coolest humans I've ever known (sorry Rob), and I am so beyond grateful that I get to be your mom. I love, admire, adore and *enjoy* you both so much, and you inspire me to be a better human every single day. I hope you read this one day (well, you better!) and understand why it's so important to find your own spark and use it to light up and lift up others as you shine bright. You two have my heart. I love you more.

My Readers

My Spark.

To the leaders who read this book, I am so excited about every single one of you! It is my greatest honor and my greatest hope that you have learned something from this book that lights your spark, and in turn, helps you to share that light with others. Let the fireworks begin!

ABOUT THE AUTHOR

Throughout her career, Jackie Insinger has brought her expertise in Cognitive Psychology and Interpersonal Dynamics to the business world as a sought-after Executive and Team Dynamics Coach. Using her research-based, action-oriented methodology, Jackie helps leaders and teams focus on unique strengths and authentic connection in order to increase performance, results, and fulfillment. Her Positive Psychology–led framework, Platinum Leadership, has been a game changer for thousands of people and businesses throughout the world. Jackie has a Psychology degree from Duke University and a Masters in Human Development and Psychology from Harvard. She is a member of both the Forbes Coaches Council and the *Harvard Business Review* Advisory Council and lives in Denver with her husband Rob, two sons Simon and Miles, and enormous Newfoundland, Hailey, aka Big Nazty.

Made in USA - Kendallville, IN
93795_9781544527109
09.03.2022 1315 .